PARENTING
with
SOUL

Nurturing Me and my Child
at Any Stage of Life

Jay Krunszyinsky

TATE PUBLISHING
AND ENTERPRISES, LLC

Published by Tate Publishing & Enterprises, LLC
127 E. Trade Center Terrace | Mustang, Oklahoma 73064 USA
1.888.361.9473 | www.tatepublishing.com

Tate Publishing is committed to excellence in the publishing industry. The company reflects the philosophy established by the founders, based on Psalm 68:11,
"The Lord gave the word and great was the company of those who published it."

Published in the United States of America

ISBN: 978-1-63268-882-8
Family & Relationships / Parenting / General
14.07.30

PARENTING
with
SOUL

Contents

Introduction

This book is written for parents, guardians, or any person placed in the role of caregiver to a child. The book outlines a new paradigm shift in parenting from old school beliefs that the world is dangerous, resources are scarce, and the world is in competition for these limited resources, to beliefs in a safe world where people are trustworthy and resources are abundant. These shifts in beliefs create a life for a child based in love and joy rather than fear. Examples of fear-based parenting are provided as the book reveals common beliefs that lead to worry and guilt in children, which prevent them of realizing their full potential. The book presents ways to develop the natural creativity and enthusiasm for life that all children possess at birth. This book prompts parents and/or caregivers to assess their level of happiness as a determining factor in their success in parenting. The book guides parents and/or caregivers down the same path to fulfilling a life purpose along with their children. The book reveals how beliefs, consciousness, and the subconscious mind play a role in creating emotional challenges or positive outcomes in one's life experiences.

When our first child was born, my wife and I felt ecstatic, stressed, amazed, and about every other emotion you can surmise. As new parents, we possessed key elements to raising our child, which remain today as well as through the birth and development of our second child. These elements are love, fun, wonderment, morality, excitement, and togetherness. We did and continue to do most activities as a family, although our children's teenage years have brought on some separation. I dedicate this book to my wife and daughters as they are living proof that the concepts and beliefs presented do support the positive development of children. In our case, we are providing witness to two lovely daughters, who are superior students and considered gifted through standardized IQ tests. Each of my daughters developed unique talents and abilities that were nurtured through my wife's unrelenting love and exploration through life's wonderments in museums, the library, and in nature. My children developed a strong love for books and reading, which account for their initial successes in school and their ability to identify and develop strong interests and desires.

Each year, our family adds special activities and rituals to celebrating the holidays, birthdays, and any other occasion. We celebrate life and successes and sometimes just celebrate for no specific reason other than we want to have fun. My wife taught our children to serve others through the church and other community organizations, such as being girl scouts. My wife knows happiness and has taught me a lot about love and happiness such as both are conscious choices to experience, and they are not based upon what others do for you. Our family also discovered the power of prayer and faith in God as our wants and desires have been answered through ways that are consistent in the messages outlined in this book. One in particular is very noteworthy. As our daughters started to get older, we noticed how the living space in our ranch-style home was becoming overrun by stuff. At the time, we knew that we wanted more space but did not know how we could get the money to pay for an architect to create drawings for a second floor, along with getting the money to construct a second floor. We loved our neighborhood, so we did not want to sell and relocate somewhere else.

The year was 2008, and the housing collapse had just occurred in the United States. My wife and I evaluated, by an external view of the world, that getting a loan and pursuing our dream of a second floor would not occur. The problem with the external world is that it does not tell the story of possibilities and the true blessings of the world. Instead, my wife and I decided to talk about what we wanted to do with friends and family. As we spoke to people, we were introduced to a contractor. This contractor also possessed the skill to create architectural drawings through computer software. He also informed us that he knew an engineer who could review and stamp the drawings for a small fee compared to the thousands of dollars that an architect would charge to develop these same drawings. At this point, we knew that we needed this same contractor to provide a bid for a second floor. While the contractor was crunching the cost numbers, I remembered hearing the desires that my wife presented about the type of kitchen and dining room she would want if we were able to renovate some day. We figured that we would have the same contractor provide these numbers as we felt an impulse to do so. After a couple of days, the contractor provided a total cost that was very reasonable, but the biggest challenge remained as we needed to find a way to secure this money.

My sister happened to work at a credit union, and to my surprise, we found a way to get an appraisal on our house that was high enough to secure all the money we needed to get the second floor and first floor renovations completed. Wait, this gets even better! After the work was completed, the interest rates took a huge drop, and we were able to refinance the loan and knock several years off of the loan at no extra monthly mortgage cost. This may appear coincidental and circumstantial to many. As time goes on in my life, I find more evidence that shows that our desires can be met by having faith in our God, ourselves, and other human beings. Once you are touched by the grace and love of others, you will start to see that your beliefs and thoughts really do determine your reality as you are what you believe. I thank my wife and children for showing me the power of love and happiness as these have nothing to do with the materials that I possess and all to do with what I choose to believe. When your children look at you with all their excitement and love for life, you truly see that this is our natural state of being, which either will remain intact or allowed to be washed away in egoistic beliefs of fear.

I wrote my initial book, *I'm Sorry*, from the perspective of how a cycle of hurt and pain causes further emotional scarring when atonement and forgiveness are not achieved. From hurt and pain, we experience negative emotions, which are not part of our natural state of well-being. We were born with enthusiasm and positive energy, with eagerness to know our world and experience life to the fullest, which is evidenced by our laughter, movement, and our love for all people, places, and events. We enjoyed colors and movement and all types of stimuli. As we started to move through our initial developmental stages of life, something started to occur to counter our love for life and our free expression and creativity. The something that began to develop is called the ego, which was our new inner voice that emerged as people in our lives started to define ground rules and beliefs that started our ride to separation from others and who we really are.

The people who helped us through our early development, many times, had the best intentions as the beliefs that were shared were to keep us safe and healthy. The rules to life and relationships began to be formed early in your life as you were told how to think and feel about others and situations and even about your own worth. As the "do that" and "don't do that" developed your ego, you became well aware of your separateness from others, which hit your emotional center of your brain and started to create fear-based feelings that emerged into your life. Family beliefs are not being judged here, only the point that thoughts and beliefs impact our state of well-being when fear is introduced from these thoughts and beliefs. Do not take me the wrong way; much of the presentation of the world impacts how we form our beliefs, yet the world we see is based upon our internal beliefs first. This may seem very foreign to you at this time, but as you read the following chapters, you will begin to see life from a new paradigm that places more control into your world.

I continue to possess many of my beliefs and values that constitute healthy relationships, such as virtuous living through acts such as love, respect, and honesty. I do acknowledge that my own beliefs play a role in my own well-being and that my initial work as a practitioner was flawed with techniques that focused on my client's ability to relive traumatic events, which only invited fear rather than healing. My use of categorization of people also placed me as someone who judged based on diagnoses and past problems. The ego was considered an essential part of one's conscious mind as this was the rational part of the mind that defined what was good and bad for you. Over the past several years, there is more and more evidence that suggests that going through hurt to gain happiness really does not work. We are all meant to be happy, but we are cutting ourselves from our happiness when we allow our ego to be the spokesperson for us.

The chapters of this book will not only help you gain understanding in why you feel the way you do but will also help you create a new story for your life and especially for your children. This is a story of love where you and your child will begin to experience the oneness with people and places that you may have even experienced at a point in time. You may have or have not known this oneness as a child and have forgotten or never knew that the world can be experienced this way. Your soul craves to experience definiteness in purpose in life where you express love, passion, and oneness with the world. Once you tap back into the love you once had with people and places in your life, you will find your happiness and abundance, which has eluded you to this point. The only way that you can be an effective parent is to regain your inner happiness even though you have been programmed to believe that happiness comes from external sources.

You may or may not know that there is more to life than the modern conveniences and time when you get on your Facebook page and play with all your virtual friends. Many of us continue to go to coffee shops, only to sit across from friends and text those not with us as the social interactions turn to isolation, away from personal contact and physical encounters with nature. You believe that one more purchase or one more social media friend will be the answer, only to find that you continue to feel empty and alone. You see the sun is out to play, yet you remain indoors to find new web pages and spend more time plugged in instead of tuned in to what your life is calling you to be. Guess what? Your children are doing or will be doing the same if you do not learn what it takes to really be alive and happy.

You have moments when you feel something is calling you when you witness acts of inspiration, love, or good-feeling stories. You know there is more to life than what you are finding on television and in the news.

So much of your time is observing the world as you see, taste, smell, hear, and touch. You have convinced yourself that the external perception of the world that you experience through these senses is reality, yet you have allowed your own intuition and internal guidance to be ignored or passed off as irrelevant to what is occurring in your life. Your internal guidance system is foolproof as you learn to trust your feelings as a feedback tool as to how well you are processing and thinking about life.

You follow so-called truths about the physical world that you live in and have accepted truths from others without question, such as where we really come from and why we exist. We rarely question how the universe really works or what the end game is for human beings. If we watch the stories unfold on the news and on other forms of media, the end game is doom and gloom. Fear is the prevailing emotion that results from news and other media that depicts the world as an unsafe and scarce place to live. Have you ever wondered why some people get everything they want while others suffer throughout their lives? The beliefs that we hold will determine what side of the aisle we end up in so you want to become very good at assessing what you believe and if the belief serves us well.

Have you ever wondered how new ideas or concepts are ever thought of when there was no resource out there that contained this information? How did Einstein and Edison think of those incredible ideas that changed the reality that was known prior to their knowledge? As you can see, reality is not solely based on your senses. There were secrets that each of the innovators of the world knew. The biggest secret was that there are infinite possibilities to what can be achieved once someone is truly tapped into their soul's desires. There is an unlimited field of knowledge beyond what is already documented or in a textbook. You have adopted beliefs that you must study these published books to gain the knowledge to be successful and happy. If this was so, why does 2 percent of the population own most of the wealth in the world? You and your children can demonstrate greatness as you both begin to develop your abilities to look to the God-given talents you possess.

When you finally shift your focus from what you are receiving from your five senses and go to the internal world of your soul and conscious mind, you can begin to tap into a new world where you are the creator of your happiness through the discovery of your purpose and calling in life. No longer will you need to emulate the life of someone else. You can create your own unique life, which meets your skills, interests, and desires perfectly and provides you with that bliss you are seeking so desperately. It is when you find the true you that you will be ready to effectively parent your child.

When you align with who you really are, you will find that your mind, body, and soul will sing with delight as you enter each day fulfilling your heart's desire and not something that you have settled for. Your child will be seen as the perfect gift, and you will naturally tend to his or her needs as your love and passion will guide your actions. This book will walk you through parenting methods but will also focus on you, the parent. Your happiness and well-being will determine the success that you have in raising your child.

Parenting involves understanding how thoughts and beliefs contribute to each of the family member's emotional state. Parents must ensure that their beliefs are promoting joy and happiness in their own lives if they are going to impart beliefs to their children that will provide positive outcomes. The external world often does not present or reflect an accurate depiction of what is possible in life. By looking to your desires and inner yearning for happiness, you and your child can set a course for an incredible journey.

Welcome to the World

Were you welcomed to the world? You may have entered life in a difficult way and were made to get on your knees, experiencing the strikes and blows that have crushed your ability to see any positive in the world. The last thing you want to hear is someone like me telling you it is time to pick yourself off the ground and get back into the real game of life. Many of you may be single parents or people who get their guts kicked in on a daily basis. You may be addicted to your drug of choice and are just waiting for a major organ to give out and ring the final bell. What I say to you is this: Who do you think you are? Do you have any clue as to who you really are? When did you start allowing your big ugly ego to dominate the true you?

Sure, you may have grown up in a family that busted you up inside and out, put little effort toward your development, or took out their emotional, physical, or even sexual crap on you. So do you really want to go down as the person that allowed the outside world to break down your eternal spirit? What you need to know is that body of yours that you think is the symbol of who you are is just an illusion of what the external world represents. That symbol is a reflection of how ugly your subconscious mind really is. And if I have not gotten your attention at this time, I want to let you in on a secret during a time when this secret may not seem popular to this world. You are not defined by a body! You are a live eternal spirit that has forgotten your true identity. When you were a baby, you knew this better than ever because you did not have any clue that you were a body. Your five senses fool you into believing that the external world defines your reality. When you are done reading this book, you are going to see and treat your life experience in a whole new way.

So I say again, "Welcome to this world," where your mind is everything and the outside world is whatever your mind has decided to show you at this stage of life. If you see ugly, you have allowed your ego to take control of your mind to project how awful others are, how you are an innocent victim, how others owe you something, and how others are to blame for your pitiful and unhappy life. As you can see, my ego can come up with harsh statements to illicit anger in you and to separate us from each other and from the world. The only problem is that the ego's only goal for us is to be miserable and die while hurting others in our path. Our children deserve so much better, and so do we!

Children are born with the understanding of love and expression. For the first year of life, a child does not know that he or she is a separate being from his or her parents. The natural instinct of a child is to be creative and experience happiness and joy. They beg us to join in their fun and joy, yet many times, parents or caretakers place them in time-outs or present consequences to them while classifying their behavior is inappropriate. Children love to touch and taste everything that comes their way as their hearts and souls sing with true delight. If you think long and hard, you were the same when you were a child, yet many parents today claim to feel the imposition of children who dare ask for some time to play, read, and sing with them. Does their wish for these things really deserve a punishment? But when you strip away the joy and love in children, their ego develops as big as the parents', and they also learn to separate from others and blame them for how they may act and feel.

Do you remember when you were filled with pure positive energy and felt the joy of life and love? You may not since you may have been cut off from the true you for a very long time. Or maybe you are a teenager and are using substances to get rid of the terrible negative emotions and isolation that you feel deep in your heart and soul. Or maybe you are contemplating suicide since the idea of releasing pain has become very appealing. Maybe your life has not come to these extremes, yet you are going through one relationship after another or working a dead-end job, wishing for retirement. In each case, you have ignored your soul's calling and have detached from who you really are. You may be experiencing these types of negative emotions while raising your child. As much as you try to keep things together, you will not be able to effectively nurture your child while you are experiencing constant and reoccurring negative emotions.

But for the moment, take some time to think back to your earliest childhood memories and how much you wanted to play, sing, read, draw, swing, run, hide, jump, hug, kiss, spin, roll, dodge, duck, dive, and nap. You should want to do this right now. Your natural state is to express love in many of these ways. We are expressive and loving people in a physical body that need connection with others and our natural world. You knew this at one time but have allowed your ego to dissuade you from engaging life in a way to bring you meaning and oneness. Through your life stages, you were taught directly or indirectly not to trust others, that your world is not a safe place, and that there is a lack of resources in the world. These beliefs have caused you to compete fervently to get what you want. As you can see, these kinds of messages are ones that will keep you centered in fear and isolated from others, yet you have convinced yourself that the world possesses these parameters and that you are justified in your actions. You surmise that your fear is justified because you claim that oneness and cooperation are false promises and that you will be tricked and deceived by others who will take from you what is rightfully yours. You need to realize how clever the ego is as you have nurtured it for quite some time.

You can probably make the case for all those times you have been taken advantage of or hurt by someone in your life as to why you are detached from others. The ego is always good at validating its stand against trust and love. We can go back and forth on the causes and effects to our lives, only to find that we can prove our side to anything if this is what we want to do. There are universal laws that state that we can attract anything that we focus our thoughts and beliefs, which makes the case that there really are no worldly truths. The only truth that transcends this world is that love is the purest and only real expression of our true self. In the end, you can justify your happiness or unhappiness. Why not choose happiness? The health and happiness of your children will be impacted by how well you attend to your well-being by learning to love yourself and those around you.

You came into this world as a happy child, seeing the world with wonderment, even if this may have been short lived. Your child will do the same. You can regain the thoughts and feelings that will bring you in line with your soul's purpose and transform your life into the experience you have always wanted but did not think was possible. This will also provide you with the complete understanding of the mechanisms that your children need to develop in order to discover their purpose in life. Neither you nor your child's future happiness will be found in the physical world. Instead, this happiness rests in the world of the mind, where both of your thoughts and feelings will guide the course of your life, even when neither of you are keeping track of what may be causing your detachment from life.

The good news is that you are in control of your happiness, and in the discovery of your soul's purpose in life. You just need to wade through some of those old beliefs and paradigms that are keeping you stuck in the mud and spinning round and round. Once you begin to deliberately choose thoughts that bring you joy and happiness, you will begin to see your life transform from the inside out.

You know that you have a strong yearning, which money, drugs, sex, and possessions cannot reach. Identification of this yearning is crucial if you are ever going to break free from the chains of your ego and become the true you. Your soul is speaking to you every day and letting you know that there is more to life than what you are experiencing. You have allowed yourself to go on autopilot and will teach your child to do the same unless you take the time to get to know who you really are and what you really want. You probably have not thought a lot about what you truly want, and if pressed, you may come up with the stuff like bigger house, cars, and other material possessions that may bring a short-term high, followed by the same empty feelings and a yearning to be more.

You may also have dismissed what you truly want as you do not see yourself as worthy or able to attain your dream. Don't feel bad about this for a great majority of people living on earth share this belief and actually believe that you have to perform certain acts, or to be born with certain attributes, to be worthy. If you base your worthiness on the opinions of others, you will hand your value over to the shifting sands of public opinion. By the fact that you are alive and breathing, your worth is immeasurable as you are gifted with the same potentiality as any other living, breathing human being. If you need proof, just look at the so-called geniuses that were labeled by others negatively, such as Albert Einstein. There are endless stories of humans who were told they were not good enough but then transformed the world.

Your child will always need to know that worthiness is not contingent upon anything or anyone. This is a given before one word is said or one action taken in life. Once you and your child believe this to be true, you both will be on the way to understanding how one gains happiness in life. Happiness does not come from others. You choose happiness as you come to believe that you are worthy of it and that your course in life is your journey and only needs to make you happy.

The innocence of children and their love for life comes as a natural part of their being. As a parent, your ability to love life and find meaning in your journey is paramount to ensuring a happy family environment. Each of us can point to circumstances and events in our childhoods that changed our innocence and produced fear. In order to effectively parent a child, you must adopt new thoughts and beliefs that reinforce that you and your child are valued and worthy of a great life. Neither of you are defined by possessions or others' opinions. You and your child were born to contribute to the world through the greatness that is found uniquely in each of you.

The Decision to Have a Child

The decision to start a family is not to be taken lightly and should not be in response to one's search for happiness. Too many new parents make the mistake of romanticizing ways that a child will bring life to their lifeless view of the world. In these cases, the birth of a child only continues the downward spiral of negative emotions. The commitment to start a family needs only to start with each parent taking responsibility for his or her own emotional well-being. Parents must start an assessment process that links thoughts and beliefs to emotions. These thoughts and emotions will only become more positive as you begin to fully engage life and come in line with your true life purpose based upon what brings you the most joy and excitement.

The preparation for having children and the game of life is an internal work that starts with looking at the person in the mirror and assessing how this person is feeling. If the answer is other than good, you will want to begin the internal journey of analyzing your thoughts and beliefs. In this assessment, you will want to link any anxiety and fear emotions to behavior that has separated you from others. The internal voice for this fear and anxiety is the ego. As long as the ego is in control, you will find every reason to blame others for your bad feelings and that there is no path to happiness. Once you begin to understand your ego, you will see how convincing the arguments can be yet how depressed you will stay. All of your fears and doubts stem from your conscious thoughts in which your ego plays throughout the day. One of the keys to happiness is the sense of connectedness and oneness with others, which are in direct opposition to the ego's wishes for you.

Let's begin with your ego's thoughts about relationships at work, at home, and with family members. If you are down on your luck and feel frustrated about your job, finances, and your relationship, your internal monologue may go something like this:

"I am tired of working for a boss and company that steals my ideas, works me long hours, and could care less about my well-being. My paycheck sucks, and I see no hope for any promotional opportunities. My wife does not understand my situation and only wants more stuff. Our bills are already beyond what we can afford, and she just sees me as someone that brings home the money. She needs to find a better-paying job. I get tired of hearing her talk about her job each day. She does not care that I stress each day and need her to help me find ways to get out of this mess. I would be in a better position in life if my parents did not divorce and leave me with no direction in life. Now, they both just guilt me into staying at a dead-end job and complain that they do not have any grandchildren."

When you add the responsibilities of taking care of a baby to the mix during a time when you are feeling defeated, your ego will speak to you about how burdensome this child is becoming and will make the case for you to serve your self-loathing and other negative emotions rather than taking care of your newborn's needs. The main issue here is that your happiness comes from your internal resources, starting with your thinking and beliefs. You were born to serve a unique and specific purpose, and your ability to answer the call to your yearning by developing a definite purpose will lead to your happiness and true place in life. In the end, you need to take heed of what you are thinking and feeling if you want to feel better and move on the path to your happiness and fulfillment.

There are universal laws that support that what you think about most of the time will come into your reality. So if your ego leads you to believe that a child is a burden, menace, or other negative connotations, then this is what you will experience in your reality. Beliefs are thoughts that you have reinforced and accepted as truth. You would be surprised how many beliefs you have and how many do not serve you well. As you walk through the ways to regain your happiness, you will also be provided powerful tools to prepare your child to see the world in a more positive and healthy light. Many parents fail to realize the importance of their state of being prior to making the decision to have children. Many believe that children will bring them happiness and attempt to fill voids in their lives. Others do not plan the arrival of children and are taken aback by announcement of the pregnancy and go into the parenting role with great fear and trepidation.

In either case, the parenting role becomes a fearful, anxious, and frustrating journey for those who are not centered in positive states of being prior to the birth of their children. This is not to say that fear, anxiousness, and frustration does not occur with the happiest of couples or single parents. The difference in people centered in well-being and people more focused in negativity is the ability to refocus into more positive emotions. Positive people understand that there are better ways to look at any situation, which keeps them calm and solution focused. Their core beliefs are that things always work out for them and that their answers to any challenge are just around the corner. Core beliefs are what determine the kind of person you currently are and how you are able to manage life challenges and setbacks. You need to be honest in your identification of your beliefs if you are to expose the ones that do not work for you.

Parents that fare well with a newborn baby are hopeful, joyful, and happy prior to the baby being born. Their natural tendency is to look at the positive aspects of their interactions and see the tasks involving the care and nurturing of the child as blessings to them. They are engaging and present in the moment and feel strong love when actively involved with their child. You know how much better you manage your life when you are feeling good versus feeling bad. You are able to see the good in others when you feel positive while you mainly see the negative side to things when feeling bad. The emotion that you pursue is the one that you actively choose. That's right! Your happiness is a choice, and making the conscious choice to be happy is a critical first step in transforming yourself to the person that you were born to be. The happier that you become, the better parent you will be. You may be asking how you can be happy by just choosing to be happy? This sounds too easy! You are partially correct; however, making this choice with emotion and passion is a good first step to rewiring your mind to adopt some new beliefs. Unhappy folks are usually not attentive to their daily thinking patterns and have not realized how many self-defeating and hopeless thoughts that they have run through their minds each day. Remember that we think over sixty thousand thoughts a day, so you can see how, over the years, you have programmed your mind and reality to present the picture that you see through your lens each day.

This is not to say that happy people do not have bad days or negative emotions. Negative emotions serve a purpose to let us know that we are experiencing something we do not want. The key is not to remain stuck in this negativity as momentum can build with the ego's assistance. We all know how to go on and rant about something or someone that ticks us off. We tend to elicit others to join in our rampage and bring up many situations and circumstances that reinforce our point of frustration, anger, hopelessness or depression. You will only be able to pick out people and situations that reinforce your point of contention, and you will have built quicksand around negative thoughts, making the escape to better thoughts very difficult. There will be discussion on ways to shift momentum from negative thinking to keep you from spiraling down too far before moving in a more positive direction.

What conversations are you having with others? What types of themes do you share in these conversations? Are you talking about the wonderment of life and the joys of your experiences, or are you speaking of the problems of the day? You may be experiencing a whole lot of bad stuff in your life, so you would find much of what is said here not relevant and a lot of hopeful bull. If you are thinking this, you have reinforced that you perceive and receive what you think about. To better receive the information in the book, you will need to find ways to open your mind to new ideas. What is there to lose but your negative emotions and experiences?

We all have shared our feelings of frustration, anger, disgust, pain, and hopelessness at one point in our lives. There is something comforting about sharing our bad feelings with others and having our views and perceptions reinforced. These conversations do serve a purpose in helping us feel somewhat better, even if we are presenting frustrations and anger. These emotions are necessary in choosing what we want based upon our unwanted experiences. The key is to move to what we want and get out of the conversations regarding the unwanted stuff. Beating the drum of what we do not want only serves the purpose of identifying what we do want as solutions can only come from moving toward what we want.

If you really take the time to evaluate your conversations about your relationships, job, finances, and health, you can begin to understand what it is that you do not want. The key is to shift to what is wanted in order to change the downward spiral, because focusing on the unwanted only brings more of it. Your mind begins to find more and more evidence of the unwanted and brings this to your experience. By shifting your focus on what is desired, you change to a positive emotional tone and outcome. We all easily dismiss what we want in life as a pipe dream that only the few ever obtain, so we continue to reinforce the unwanted situations in our lives. You must start by allowing yourself to dream about what you want and let yourself off the hook from trying to figure out the details of how your dreams can come true. Until you learn about how the world will bring you the people and circumstances to make your dreams a reality, you need to start to catch yourself when you are in conversations that only focus on complaints without solutions. Spend more time looking at pictures and resources that depict those things that bring you joy and excitement, and see yourself as if you already are participating in your dream. This will go far to reinforcing what you want to the subconscious mind, which will believe that your attainment of your dream is true and will start to work to guide you to the path of realizing this dream.

By now, your ego has to be telling you that this nonsense has nothing to do with raising children and that happiness is not a choice. The ego will also recite the tale regarding how life is a struggle and the game is rigged, so you need to take what you can get from life and teach your child how tough and brutal life and the world truly is. If this is your vantage point, you have suffered in life and need to find a different path to move to a better perspective of the world if you ever want your child to embrace the world in a positive way. Fear is the only emotion that can come from a world that depicts everyone as the enemy. Fear also can be disguised as apathy, anger, frustration, and other negative emotions. So if you have disengaged from people and places due to viewing the world in negative ways, you also fall into the fear-based crowd where the ego stands tall to keep you at odds with life to ensure that you never find ways to true happiness.

To get to a point where you can positively nurture your children through their development, you must adopt a paradigm shift. This new paradigm must encompass a parenting and world view that inspires you and your children to follow your life's calling based upon your interests and talents. You most likely were taught that life is a struggle and you need to compete in a very unsafe world to survive. You most likely heard that the rich are the only ones who get the breaks and that the poor keep getting poorer with the middle class becoming extinct. The world reinforces your ego by showing you evidences of these beliefs on a twenty-four-hour news and entertainment cycle on the distraction machine known as a television. If you recite these thoughts and believe them, you will experience all the lack and scarcity of resources that you present with the emotion of fear. If you live from a new paradigm and teach new beliefs of trust, abundance, and love to your children, your family will break free from the captivity that you feel and experience.

Your children will be born creative and must be allowed to expand this creativity if they are going to find their purpose in life. Children tested at age two have shown to possess a very high creative brain capacity, which is around 95 percent but dwindles down to 2–4 percent by the time they reach age seven. This creativity comes from the subconscious mind, which is free from limiting beliefs at this stage in life. Mozart was writing music prior to age five and wrote his first opera at age eleven. Hungarian-born John von Neumann was memorizing pages from the phone book as an eight-year-old. With an IQ around 210, Kim Ung Yong started university courses at age three. There are many accounts of child prodigies who have shown great intelligence and creative abilities that were recognized by their parents and allowed to progress and be reinforced through exposure to more of their area of interest. In a way, these children were able to tap into their creative minds unimpeded by limitations and doubt. They were encouraged to think outside the norm and present new and creative works to the world.

Parents, caretakers, and others who come in contact with the child share their beliefs regarding life with the child. When children are provided beliefs that illicit strong emotions, they adopt the beliefs to gain a sense of belonging and conformity. Many times, adults unintentionally send messages to children that produce fear and negativity. These messages can come in many forms that squash dreams and the imagination of children. In attempts to be helpful, adults allow their insecurities to be the basis for sharing why a young person's dreams are not realistic. These same adults only see a child fitting in a certain box in the world. If you follow any of the great achievers and happy folks of your generation and of past generations, you will find that they did not conform to the masses and even appeared different and eccentric in their approaches to life. In our attempts to fit the mold of the society, we have lost ourselves in the process and have led our children to mediocrity at best in many circumstances.

You as a parent or caretaker of children must gain insight into your own limiting beliefs to be able to raise a child to meet his or her full potential. If you feel less than good and lost as a person, you will experience a near-impossible task when it comes to fully engaging your child at each level of development. There is a big difference between raising a child to develop his or her full potential and putting a roof over a child's head and providing three square meals. The latter is a limiting belief of a good percentage of parents who look at child development with broad strokes and miss the important details of each present moment that they spend with their children. These moments are life blessings as each encounter is a most sacred opportunity to share love and creativity. Your ego will attempt to convince you that your parenting role is limited to providing solely for their basic needs. When you feel negative emotions, you will find it easier to separate from your children by sticking them in front of a television, sending them to their bedrooms, and speaking to them only when you are upset and presenting directives their way.

Through their interactions with adults, children absorb the messaging from many of the adults during their initial developmental stages. Your childhood messages and experiences have led you to the beliefs that you respond to each and every day both consciously and subconsciously. Your emotional states are a direct result to the beliefs you hold. When you feel negative emotions, you are responding to beliefs that are controlled through an ego response to people, places and circumstances. The ego response is to avoid responsibility and/or separate from others. You and your children's ability to find meaning in life centers on how well you can focus on your desires and joy while limiting your time focused on what is not wanted. Your view of the world and the people in it has a direct influence on your happiness. Many parents develop their view of the world based upon the media and other external forces, which tends to take a fear-based approach to life where human potential is limited. Until parents make a shift to beliefs that foster infinite potential in their children, their approach to parenting will not promote the full potential and creativity in their children.

Parenting with a Paradigm Shift

There are many resources on raising and developing children. Many of these resources are more reactive in nature by presenting methodology on ways to manage problems. The old paradigm of managing children is that we wait for problems, give them a diagnosis, and provide instructions on management of the diagnosis. Once diagnosed, the parent receives instruction on behavioral modification techniques and/or was provided powerful medications. This may sound harsh, but children deserve much better than this. When we look at children as problems, we are not parenting from the right perspective, nor are we parenting from the right thinking and emotions. Parents that come to therapists and psychiatrists are usually at their wits end and have very little perspective left in the tank, especially one who views their child as a joy. They have allowed themselves to get so focused on the negative aspects of their child that they are convinced that the child has a conduct and/or emotional problem.

Kids are not born problem children, and their natural state is one of love and joy. Children act in ways that are learned to get their needs met. Period! Children are reinforced to act in the ways they present to others. Parents very seldom take responsibility for reinforcing their children's behavior unless the behavior is considered good or appropriate. Children want their parents' time and attention and find ways to gain these by behaving in ways that best achieve their objectives. The time parents spend with children to develop through the initial stages of life is a critical parenting window to determine the ability of children to thrive physically, socially, and educationally.

The paradigm shift you make must take into account that your view of your child is based upon your beliefs and not always the truth. This may sound crazy to you, but your mind will only see what you program it to see. This is why your stability and emotional well-being is critical prior to managing children. If you see the world as unsafe, unfair, and lacking resources, you will pass these same views and beliefs to your children. Even though your friends, family, and the media may reinforce this view, you must work to adopt new beliefs that bring hope and joy to your life. The paradigm shift includes switching from a belief system of fear and doubt to one of love and hope. The only way to be an effective and nurturing parent is to adopt beliefs of hope and joy in the world. Why else would you have brought this precious life into the world? Your child will live up to your beliefs and expectations in many cases, so you'd want to set the stage early for love, hope and joy to be the prevailing themes in your home.

You say that this sounds like a pipe dream or maybe you say that believing in love, joy, and hope is not in the cards for you. The second part of this paradigm shift is that the first ingredient that you need for these thoughts and beliefs to become your reality is for you to possess a strong desire for what you want that includes strong feelings of love and excitement. The second ingredient is to imagine that you are in possession of what you truly desire or want and allow these strong positive emotions to accompany these thoughts and images. Your subconscious mind becomes activated when messages are presented to it with strong emotions. When you think about what you desire and vividly picture it with strong positive emotions, the subconscious mind goes into action to bring your desires to your reality. Your ability to define and visualize what your soul desires is part of this process. If you connect with your yearning, your heart will get jump started and your subconscious mind will go to work to bring you to this calling.

You have to know that you are a restless soul that may turn to addictions to attempt to sooth that restlessness that is stirring within you. You spend hours on the television or computer, attempting to zone out this restlessness and continue to feel unsatisfied and empty inside. You may turn to drugs and alcohol to temporarily take away your feelings of fear and anxiety. You know this is true if you really look honestly at your life. These soft addictions or distractions are very common today as people in society are not able to find what they are looking for in the world. What they are looking for is what their true purpose or yearning is in life. This yearning must be attended to if you are going to find the fulfillment of your life and true happiness. This yearning will lead you to your purpose in life and will also be a roadmap as to where your child will need to navigate as they develop into adults.

How you identify what you are yearning is not always apparent. Many people start with material possession or a career choice. A yearning is much bigger than that. You want to ask yourself, what does what you think you want lead to in your life? For example, if you want a million dollars, you can ask what this would lead to. You may answer, "A big house" and "My bills paid off." If you ask what that leads to, you may say freedom. Then you may say that freedom leads to doing what you always wanted, which was to be a writer. If taken further, you may find that being a great writer leads you to being a major influence on the world. As you see, your yearning can take you to some big places, all that are achievable once you rewire your brain to accept the challenge joyfully and hopefully.

To identify what your purpose in life will be usually can be found by what you truly enjoy doing, something that excites you and brings out your passion. Money and material things are temporary wants we all have, yet the obtainment of any material want is a short-lived joy and does little to bring true meaning to you. Being able to do activities that you are passionate about is what really sustains your joy and happiness in life! You may be passionate about telling stories, painting, writing, or building stuff. The best first step is to get involved in these activities in any manner you can to light the flame of your passion. With the internet and other great resources, you can find people, places, and activities where your talents can be discussed and progressed.

Once you have identified all the things that you want in your life, you will begin to spend time dreaming and thinking as though they have already occurred and basking in the joyful and hopeful feelings that these visualizations provide. Taking time to think about what you want each day as though they have occurred will start to provide your subconscious with new thoughts that will be accepted as your new belief patterns. These exercises along with statements of appreciation for the people, places, and things that you currently possess in your life will jump-start your brain to move your emotions from negative to more hopeful and happy ones. With this new paradigm, you now bear the responsibility of knowing that your thoughts and beliefs are what make up your reality, so you need to be more aware of those thoughts that are running through your mind. Although it is virtually impossible to monitor each and every thought you think, you can monitor how you are feeling throughout your day, which will let you know if you are slipping back into old negative-thinking patterns.

There is science that backs the importance of thoughts and emotions to your outcomes in life, so this is a critical part to your personal and parenting development. This science presents a correlation of your thoughts and beliefs to your present reality. Quantum physics experiments show that particles and matter do not react until we consciously observe them. Further research has gone further to show that our thoughts and emotions actually change the molecular structure of objects. This science, along with the psychology of the mind, reinforces the notion that what we draw our thoughts and attention to become our reality. This may sound far-fetched and out of a science fiction movie! The important part to take from this is that we do observe more of what we focus our attention to. So if we are feeling blue and depressed, we tend to notice sad and depressing themes. When we feel happy and excited, we begin to notice positive themes in our lives. No matter what is actually going on in the mental or physical world, we tend to bring about what we think about for this is our point of focus.

There are going to be times when the world beats you up inside, and you will fall back into negative-thinking patterns. The next skill to develop is your ability to go back to a neutral state of being when you experience frustration, anger, resentment, being overwhelmed, and depression. If you are like me, once you start the down-hill spiral into the negative arena, the momentum only grows as we tend to recruit others to share our points of misery. The biggest contributor to the downward spiral is our ability to focus on the specifics of what we don't like or want, which only keeps us justified in our position and entrenched in our negativity. And since like attracts like, there are more than enough people out there feeling down and out who will join our chorus.

In sports, coaches know a lot about momentum, and they try to ride that momentum as long as possible. The coaches on the losing end also know to take a time-out to slow down the force, which is a true phenomenon. Your time-out will consist of making a conscious effort to take the specifics out of the current thoughts that you are thinking and switching them to thoughts that are broader and will carry less intensity. For example, if you are thinking and replaying specific ways that someone has treated you by stating how you reacted or could have reacted, you will want to make one broad statement about the situation. You may think, "I did not like how I was treated today." From this statement, you may need to remain on a broad and general thinking pattern and state. "I do not know what I did to deserve this." After a few broad thoughts, the skill development you will need is to be able to slip some broad statements that demonstrate more hopeful thinking, such as, "Most of my day went well before this person said what she did" and "Things always look better the next day."

From more hopeful broad statements, you will want to move your momentum to the positive direction. You can think thoughts about the things that did go well that day and move to the things that you appreciate in your life and to your positive attributes and all the things that you are on your way to obtaining, which you will discover in finding your purpose in life. From each step discussed in the chapter, you'd want to keep a small journal and write what you want, your true desires and purpose in life, what you appreciate, and your positive attributes to remind you of where you need to focus to move to a positive conscious thought process. Initially, you will not be able to switch gears naturally, so you will need your journal to keep you on track to move your thinking to happier dreams and aspirations.

With this journal, you can also start to write how you feel throughout the day and those thoughts that contributed to that emotion. This will help you to identify what beliefs you currently hold that are keeping you from experiencing the love and joy that are part of the true you. The more beliefs that you can identify that are causing you hurt and suffering, the more insight you will gain to begin to review and dispel these thoughts and replace them with loving and empowering ones that are more based in truth and happiness. You must remember that your ego will not ever go away and will attempt to draw you back to your old thinking patterns, which will keep you separated and isolated from others. The road to happiness and fulfillment for you and your child relies on your persistence and fortitude through this process.

Once you begin to experience the obtainment of some of the stuff that you want, you will be able to satisfy the ego's craving for individual gain, yet you will begin to shift your focus to what you want and desire. This will also serve your ego as the ego loves reinforcement. That is why you must experience the success of this new way to approach your desires in life. You will find joy and happiness, which will reinforce and keep the ego happy as you achieve individual goals. You will need your ego's assistance in attaining those initial test run items that you want until you begin to transcend the material wants and make your transformation to the real you.

Your subconscious mind also loves imagery tied to strong emotion as this will leave strong mental blueprints as how you desire to live, as if these desires are currently being played out in your life. Your subconscious mind does not understand past and future events and sees all messaging as now. If you start to visualize your desires and gather visual depictions of the things that you want, you can take time each day and see yourself as possessing or participating in these visual depictions as if they are occurring right now. Children do this all the time until they are told that they are living a pipe dream and that they need to wake up to reality. Instead of their desires and dreams becoming the blueprint of their subconscious mind, the doubt and fear of not achieving their dreams became more prevalent, which the subconscious mind also obliges and makes part of their reality.

Once your subconscious mind gets new pictures and beliefs that are accompanied by strong positive emotions for a consistent period of time these new beliefs will become the predominant ones that will guide your actions. Taking time each week to visualize your dreams as real; you will begin to change the current course where you wake up feeling uninspired and depressed. You will start your day with an eagerness and excitement to get going and to take actions toward your dreams and desires. This is when the magic of your life will begin, and you will find yourself meeting people, finding places, and receiving impulses to move in the direction of your soul's yearning. Still sound too incredible and not possible? These concepts and beliefs are not easily adopted if your current beliefs continue to look at dreams as impossible and life as a tough road. You, like many, do not see living a dream as a simple process and want more of a step-by-step guide to success. If these guides were truly the way to go, would not more folks be able to achieve their true aspirations and dreams?

The path to your dreams is not cookie cutter or "one size fits all" as the way to your dreams is more of a synchronous journey. On your path, you will start with identifying and visualizing your dream or any desire or want that is important to you. Share your excitement with as many people as you can. You will want to talk about what you want to do and demonstrate what your talents are as you attract more and more people that get excited about your desire. The only action that you need is to be able to get out and about and share what you love to do with as many people as you can. From these efforts, the dreaded "how to" will begin to form as people will direct you in the directions necessary to get on the path to your dream.

The final part to your own personal journey towards happiness and joy is when the uncertainty of your calling in life begins to take shape. As you encounter others that share in your interests, you will gain ideas on ways that your ideas can manifest into products and/ or services for others. As you gain a clearer picture of how your talents and desires can be developed, you must make the conscious decision to feed your subconscious mind images, thoughts, and emotions that create positive life outcomes for your emerging purpose in life. You want to visualize the clearer picture of where your desires and yearning takes you by continuing to share with others of like-mindedness until you come to a point where you know exactly where your path is leading. This moment of clarity comes when you allow your subconscious mind to communicate this to you. You must allow this to happen by placing faith in the universe that happiness will reveal your next steps in the process. This may sound very foreign to you as we are all taught that we must take action first and then we will have time for happiness. I say to you with certainty that the opposite is true. You need to find happiness within yourself first, and then you will be guided on the next steps to take for you and your child.

Once you begin to discover your purpose in life, your actions become more deliberate, and you will feel more relevance from what you can contribute to others with your talents and passions. Your connections will increase as you gain confidence in the path you are heading. Relevance and connection are needs that human beings need to have meaning and purpose in life. We also have the need for change (uncertainty) along with certainty. If we do not have any change in life, we easily become bored, so change is a need for us. Many who claim to hate change are not happy and feel better about the predictability of their unhappiness rather that the possibilities that change may bring. Constant change is not what we need as we become unstable emotionally when we do not gain certainty out of the change for we need mastery in our life also. Too many children grow up getting these needs met by committing crimes, bullying, and other antisocial behaviors. These acts bring certainty, uncertainty, relevance, and connection during the abusive or violent act at hand. If you do not find positive and meaningful ways to satisfy needs, you will meet them in dysfunctional ways. Your ego will help you devise ways to project and justify your frustrations and anger.

The final two needs that you and your child possess are paramount in defining your happiness and success in living life. These are the need to grow as a person and to make a contribution to the world. These last two needs go hand in hand, with having definiteness in purpose and a positive conscious approach to living. These final needs along with a new belief system will bring certainty out of uncertainty and connection with others from a point of compassion and love. Your relevance will be established from these connections and your path to your true purpose in life.

You may be wondering how you would find your purpose. You need to go back in time and look to what you wanted to do more than anything else. What could you spend your life doing each day that would bring out your greatest joy, excitement, achievement, and fulfillment? Better yet, stick to what would bring you the most fulfillment, as many look to high-paying careers as what they think their purpose is when, really, this is the furthest from the truth. If you are stressed each and every day and make a ton of money, will you be happy? There are many wealthy people who only feel misery as their stress levels go through the roof, which translates to health problems and other conflicts in their relationships. A true life purpose is performing something that can fulfill you without devouring you. You can lose track of time and never feel fatigued from performing or engaging in activities that your soul calls you to do. What did you dream of being as a kid? Write down all the stuff you wanted to do or become, and find some common themes and activities that come from your list of dreams. Your yearning and purpose most likely lie in the commonalities of these dreams.

The path you take toward well-being and happiness will be a good guide for what your children will need to follow in order to develop their life purposes and full potentiality where they picture a world of peace, harmony, and life fulfillment. If these messages sound more like fantasy to you, all I have to say is that your ego remains in the forefront of your thinking and emotions. Your doubts and other negative emotions stem from this ego and the beliefs that you have adopted in your life. If you are going to be all that you can be for you and your child, you need to quit making excuses and projecting blame on others and get to your life purpose already. Time goes quickly, and you do not want to be someone who reflects back on all their regrets and should haves, could haves, and would haves.

Your ability to find your path to happiness is of primary importance prior to bringing a child into the world. Parents that can assess their thoughts and beliefs in honest and responsible ways find that their negative emotions are linked to fear and positive emotions to love. Parents that can replace fearful thinking and beliefs with joyful and hopeful ones make the connection that happiness is a choice rather than an emotion resulting from circumstances in life. Parents that choose happiness internally through the use of visualization, appreciation, and the identification of positive personal attributes turn around the momentum of negativity. You will start to realize that the presentation of the external world is a result of your internal thoughts and beliefs. Many of us have been taught that our outcomes in life are limited based upon factors in the external world. Life possibilities become greater as we realize that we contribute to the positive and negative outcomes in our lives through our beliefs and thoughts. As you focus more on your desires and what your soul yearns, your excitement will lead you to the people, places, and circumstances that will define your passions in life changing directions.

My Ego and My Fear

You may be asking yourself, "What is this ego, and why is it so bad?" Sigmund Freud spoke of our psyche and that there were three parts that controlled our minds. They were the impulsive id; the straight and narrow superego; and the mediator of the two, the ego. From the psychological perspective, the ego is our conscious thought, which drives our thoughts, emotions, and actions. The problem with the ego is that it derives much of its primal fears from the hidden beliefs of the subconscious where there is no differentiation from what is true or actually false. As information is fed to you in your life, the subconscious becomes a recorder that takes in all information that you have received through your senses and manages this data as if all were based out of truth. The only way this is altered is when you consciously evaluate the information and consciously refute the information. This means that all messages from people, television, and other media has shaped much of what you believe, even if you do not consciously realize it. This can help to explain why you feel negative emotions out of the blue when you are triggered by external stimuli.

The ego is the part of your mind that attempts to explain and rationalize why you feel the way you do. Your ego reinforces negative emotions as a way to protect you from further harm to your psyche. Talk about being trapped in an indefinite loop of negativity. The ego convinces you to remain separate from others by making the cases for looking out for number one and striking first before getting hurt by others. To see the ego's work, just look at all the people who isolate from others and lack trust and fellowship with others. If you look at the increase in depression, addictions, and other psychiatric disorders, you can see that the ego has become powerful in convincing many to fear the world and to remain separated from others, resulting in emotional states of emptiness and hopelessness. You may exclaim in a very loud voice, "I am not afraid of anything!" To exclaim this is to admit the opposite. All the negative emotions, such as your guilt, doubt, worry, anxiety, depression, anger, frustration, rage, etc., have originated from fear.

To parent a child, you need to understand the role of the ego and what the real truth is about the world. The technology today is very impressive and alluring as we can now witness in real time the news that unfolds presenting the most intense, disturbing, and explosive entertainment through our media. The intense programming that you and your child are exposed to with smart phones, movies, television, and the other forms of computers have created the images, emotions, and sounds to develop an ego belief system that is more destructive to the human psyche than ever. The twenty-four-hour news cycle and end-of-the-world theme entertainment has helped to develop an ego that views the world as a dangerous place and a world heading for the end of times. The ego tells you that no one is to be trusted, you must be ready to do battle with everyone, and that there is lack throughout the world. When you believe that life is a struggle to obtain any resource, your ego makes the case for you to get what you can get and protect it with your life. Did I miss anything? Of course, there is the mantra that the rich get richer, the poor get poorer, and that a world war could start at any time and wipe us all out. There we go! The ego has set the stage to keep us all fearful, so we never fully enjoy another day of our lives. Then our more uplifting tales involve reality television that shows us how to be irresponsible and get paid well to do so.

Many parents have allowed their children to get lost in a world that broadcasts messages to them both consciously and subconsciously. There is no coincidence that more children are demonstrating emotional disturbances and are developing narcissistic and sociopathic personalities. When beliefs and messages that say life is a joke, that life does not matter, that life is about what I get, that life is about what I take, or that life is about the drug I take, run through the minds of adults and children, then the ego has landed. At this point, you may think that there is evidence to support this ego view as there are facts that can back up the claims of gloom and doom. The point to be made is that there are facts that can point to any perspective that you adopt. If you really want to live a life of love and joy with your child, you need to wrestle your ego to the ground and isolate it more and more, day by day, moment by moment. To do this, you must evaluate beliefs that make you feel bad and evaluate them consciously. I know this sounds like a whole bunch of psychological mumbo jumbo. All this means that you need to start taking inventory of what you believe and think when you are feeling bad.

This may sound like a ton of work to do. Start peeling back the onion of thoughts and beliefs, and you will soon find the origins of your negative thoughts. Most came from beliefs and messages that produced fear in your life. You were also given many messages of what not to do, which only furthered your negative thinking instead of focusing on wanting to be happy. To make the turn to a more joyous and happy life and to possess the skills to impart on your child, you must slow down the downward spiral of negative thinking. You can only do so by adopting some new beliefs. Let's start with your beliefs about people. How do you view the human condition? Do you believe that people are good and trustworthy? Do you see others as productive and caring individuals? Do you think of the world as safe? For many people, these questions are hard to affirm as the messaging throughout time has been to the contrary. Until you can change your beliefs to see others as loving and trustworthy, you will experience issues with your relationships as you will tend to see faults that will reinforce this point of focus. Until you realize how the subconscious and conscious mind come together to create the world, you will remain lost in a fearful world that keeps you from experiencing the joy experienced with others. What about the dangers out there? When you make the conscious decision to trust and love others, your natural intuition will guide you from danger and attract people and places that correspond with your new thoughts and beliefs. Like I said, this is a paradigm shift but one that is backed by psychology and science.

To make this more simplified, you have a choice of either focusing on love or fear when dealing with others. Many of those who are victimized or harmed by others are focused in fear and all the emotional derivatives of fear such as anger, hate, rage, and frustration, worry, and anxiety. The person who runs off of rage is more in tune to take out his/her rage on someone who is emulating a negative emotion even when these emotions differ. The abuser and victim may be viewed as not sharing a common bond, yet each resonates in similar ways with the emotion of fear. The law of attraction gives scientific and spiritual reasons for this phenomenon and is backed by psychological research. This is not to say that any one person can eliminate the emotion of fear in their lives, nor should he or she. This speaks to the person who resonates fear as a baseline emotion. Fear is an emotion that serves us well when we notice that danger is present or that certain acts increase our risks in life.

To adopt new relationship beliefs, you will need to address old beliefs when they surface. You will know they are surfacing when you start to think that people are idiots, can't be trusted, only break your heart, rip you off, conspire against you, and many other ego thoughts. Thoughts that someone is taking advantage of you or talking behind your back are an indication that you will want to challenge your old belief system and show love and kindness toward them. This action will serve two purposes. The most important purpose is that it helps to strengthen your new belief system that people possess love. Secondly, these actions will produce an automatic shift in your relationship as the other person's perception of you will change. This change, many times, ignites compassion.

When you show love to someone, you are really showing love to yourself. This brings us to one of the most important guidelines that will help you gauge your progress with your ego in the area of relationships. When you look at another person, your view of them is a reflection of your view of yourself that has just surfaced from your subconscious. This alone can help you track what beliefs you hold that hurt your relationships, including the one you have with you. Even more important, these are really the views that you fear in yourself. The ego does not want you to know this as this would shake the ego's core survival system. The ego wants to ensure that you do not track the source of your relationship issues. In essence, you are looking into a mirror when you address relationships in your life. The more love you see in the world, the more love you have for you.

What does all that mean? Your view of the world and people in it are a representation of all of your beliefs, especially about yourself. This psychological paradox is extremely difficult to grasp as each of us can make claim that people are annoying, selfish, and many other adjectives. The challenge for you is to see which of these adjectives do not describe you or is a possibility for you at some point in your life. The important point to understand is that your treatment of another person does indicate your level of love for another human being and yourself. When you fully love you, you can only see others with love. When beliefs that produce fear are no longer the front runners in your mind, you begin to view others in a very different manner as your acceptance and tolerance are heightened. If you want to test how much you love yourself, spend time with the one person who has a history of bringing out your negative emotions. When you can see them with love and compassion, you are on the right path. Your relationship with others starts with your relationship with yourself!

Your ego also lets you know about scarcity and lack in your life, especially in the areas of your health and finances. Not only does the twenty-four-hour news cycle and media show gloom and doom footage, they also let us know how much our health is suffering and how weak the country is economically. If you do not consciously dispel these messages, your subconscious will adopt these messages as beliefs and will work to make these issues your reality. Do you think it is a coincident that people who feel helpless, hopeless, frustrated, and depressed usually also experience poor health and finances? We can get in one hell of a rut when we subscribe to what the world is telling us to believe and on how to live our lives. This is also why so many research studies show that when someone believes they received a medication to treat their illness, they get better even when the medication was a placebo. In the area of health, your subconscious mind is responsible for all the body's involuntary health processes and maintenance of trillions of cells and organ functions of the body.

More and more research is showing that your belief system about your health does impact your well-being. As a parent, you need to understand the importance of positive emotions and beliefs in regards to your health and well-being. Your ability to share this wisdom will be a fantastic gift to impart on your child. Although a physician's care is an important part of your and your child's health, the positive beliefs about health and well-being will contribute to the overall health of both of you. If you see yourself as in perfect health and adopt this as a core belief, you will soon begin to see this become part of your reality as long as you monitor the types of interactions that you encounter regarding health. If you noticed, more disease and medication advertisements are being broadcasted with a positive correlation of an increase in cases of disease and medical issues. This is not an indictment on medicine and doctors. This is a statement regarding the power of the subconscious messaging and the relationship between negative emotions and poor health.

Your ego contributes to the feelings of stress and fear by making the case that everyone gets sick and that cancer is a big risk for people in your family. If you dread that you may get a certain illness, then you are calling on your subconscious to bring this into your reality. More and more studies are showing that emotional fears and stress contribute to most of the medical problems that human beings face. You have been told that your heredity and your diet and exercise regime impact your health. I am here to tell you that any of this is true if you truly believe it to be so. How confused are you now? Your beliefs are the core of what you are, and your emotions determine how well you are expressing the true you. The more positive and happy you feel, the more that you are in love with life and others. The more miserable you feel, the more your ego is in control, resulting in poor relationships and more health-related problems.

Science, medicine, religion, and psychology are all catching up to the fact that your conscious and subconscious minds are what guide your emotional, physical, and spiritual well-being. You have the opportunity to begin a new journey in life with a new way to look at your world and your place in it. This will not only transform you to someone who finds their true purpose and meaning on this earth but also provide you with the tools to do the same for your child. Making the paradigm shift from a victim of circumstance to a powerful human being in control of life outcomes promotes a great sense of freedom. This shift in world views provides a person with the ability to control one's health and happiness and can really place you on an even playing field with your ego. Are you ready to stop blaming others and build the strength to rebuild your mind to become the strong, free, joyful, and loving person that you were before the barrage of negativity that the world fed you from the time you were born until now? Fear does not go away easy, so you must be able to manage setbacks and find the inner strength to challenge the status quo and old beliefs by stepping out of your comfort zone. This may mean that you need to get off the couch or computer chair and find people, places, and activities that will introduce you to others who will push you to be the best that you can be and who will honestly let you know when you are being a "baby." To be an effective parent, you should no longer be the victim of circumstances in life.

The only way you can reinforce new beliefs about relationships and your health is to engage in events that support social interaction and physical activity as a transformation process. This process will consist of engaging the community to establish and reinforce new beliefs of loving relationships and good health. You could engage in activities that would combine the two areas of your belief system, such as taking walks with friends or joining a fitness club. The point is to start with a positive belief about people and health and to go out and experience people and activities that reinforce your belief. The more positive experiences you have that include the emotions of happiness, love, joy, and fun, the more that your subconscious will play these new recordings as your new truths. You will find that your emotions will begin to brighten, and you will start to see others and the world in a new light. As you learn to anticipate positive occurrences with people and places prior to the actual encounters, you will find that these experiences will play out even more positively for you. Using the same visualization and strong emotional responses as mentioned previously will help the subconscious mind receive these new activities as beneficial in your belief system.

One way to preplan your day is to break it down into activity segments and take time prior to any of the segments to visualize how you want the interactions and outcomes to occur. See the happy and fun exchanges along with the peace, harmony, and cooperation from visualization accompanied with great positive emotions. This helps the subconscious to take in the information as if this segment has already occurred and will provide you with a better chance for a positive experience. You can start each day by visualizing a scene from your bed of an enjoyable breakfast experience. You could imagine yourself making a great breakfast and having a fun and happy conversation with your spouse. Feel the joy and smell and taste the great breakfast in your visualization. You can do this same preplanning technique on the car ride to and from work and each part of a working day. Many successful people get into the proper state of mind before a presentation by visualizing their talk and seeing the crowd enthused and engaged in their presentation. By visualizing segments of your day ahead of time, you allow yourself time to arrive in a positive state of mind to ensure better interactions and experiences.

The key is to see the world as a child all over again and to begin an internal dialogue that treats each encounter with new wonderment and excitement. You want to see each new day as another chance of meeting or encountering the countless possibilities to happiness, which will lead you to your true purpose and destiny in life. The innocence of children is a wonder to behold as they show sheer enjoyment from riding a bike, playing in the mud, rolling down a hill, chasing a friend in tag, greeting their friend coming out of their house, singing songs, and anticipating what the family has planned next for them. Even a child with cancer provides that smile and love that comes natural to them as the child sees everyone and everything as comfort and love.

You need to get back in love with life and especially with you. You can never share love with others until you fall back in love with you. After you spend time engaging others and participating in activities to reinforce your new beliefs, you must take time to appreciate what gifts and qualities that you possess that make you that special you. This may not be easy if you still have old beliefs of being unworthy, average, unattractive, stupid, and other negative images received directly or indirectly. Even if you can't identify your positive attributes easily and genuinely, you must reflect on your life to discover your positive characteristics and abilities if you are going to get your mind back to where you begin to live life proactively. Your child is worth you being the best you as this will contribute to your child developing to be their best.

The ego will tell you that you do not have time for this psychological crap and that your child's welfare has nothing to do with your happiness or unhappiness. Your ego will tell you that you do not need anyone else telling you what to do and that you made it through life to this point. Like stated previously, any statement that you make and believe will become your reality. Again, the question remains. "Does your reality make you happy?" If you can say that it honestly does, then you have a belief system fully in place that supports love and joy. If you cannot honestly say that you are happy, you will need to challenge that old ego of yours by taking some emotional and behavioral risks to fully engage the world and allowing yourself to be embraced by others. Even when your beliefs on health and your relationships serve you better, old fears such as lack will creep into your life as a parent. Financial crisis and medical emergencies can throw your entire system back to the old patterns of thoughts and beliefs in no time at all. The worry of financial resources or lack thereof is one of the most common parenting barriers that bring much stress and conflict, creating a downward spiral to relationships and health.

One of the biggest challenges that a parent faces is how to meet financial obligations. In many two-parent, one-parent, or in other caretaker configurations in the home, financial lack is a primary belief. Parents worry constantly about financial affairs. They carry additional beliefs that only the rich get ahead, the rich get richer, the poor get poorer, and that there is too much competition out there to get ahead. If you consider what has been stated about how the subconscious mind regards everything as the truth, you will understand how lack of financial resources has become your reality. This is not to say that if you, all of a sudden, make the claim that you are abundantly rich, that a sack of money will appear at your door. Making the claim that you have abundance is a step in the right direction for abundance consists of more than just material wealth. What happens too often with many folks is their inability to see what is right in front of their noses. The issue is that many of us look at what we do not have and complain about not having enough. The subconscious is a grantor of our wishes, so your life reel may show you more evidence of your lack each and every day.

Again, your focus on any issue in your life has a positive side and negative one. So when you flip your statement that you do not have enough, you start to state an appreciation for what you do possess. One of the biggest "aha" moments that people encounter is when they take inventory of what they possess. There are many households in the USA that have multiple televisions, high-speed Internet, cell phones, at least one car, and a place to house these items along with the food and clothing necessary to live each and every day. When we start to appreciate what we often take for granted, we make a shift in our belief of lack in our life. The ego wants you to envy others for what they have and to never be satisfied with what you have. Have you ever noticed how after you purchase something you want, the item loses its perceived value to you over time and that you continue to see lack in your life?

To change the belief about material stuff and finances, you must change your view of abundance and lack. Many of us equate riches with money when the word *abundance* means so much more. Abundance in nature is always evident as plants always overproduce to ensure that there is an abundance of its outpouring. This can be said about everything in nature except human beings. For some reason, we believe that we should possess abundantly without bringing forth our own abundance of substance that is within our soul. This abundance is your internal unlimited potential to create and develop from the gifts and talents that you possess. This is where your yearning and purpose in life is waiting to be tapped. Your abundant gifts and talents were meant to serve others in ways that contribute to the higher good of society. To give of yourself to others is to give back to you. Many people think that receiving from others brings them joy and fail to experience the fulfillment that giving and serving the needs of others brings. Not only does this bring you fulfillment, your acts will also reward you with many forms of abundance such as love, relationships, and material substance. When your services are highly desired, you begin to set the stage for the return of many forms of abundance.

The knowledge that you have infinite possibilities to how your talents and purpose will develop and take form is why you need to rest assure that you will always have abundance in your life. Your life will lack nothing other than the limitations that you place on yourself. Your ego is just chomping at the bits to say, "This all sounds good, but how does this put food on the table and pay the rent and utility bills?" Again, the point to understand is that the ego's view only shows the problem and the fear that reinforces the issue of lack. The idea of a life purpose from love looks at the possibilities, which is the path to happiness gained from discovering what you are called to do in life. If you only knew how close you are to taking your passions in life and fulfilling your dreams. There are numerous examples of people taking those activities they so enjoy and creating a life where they get to perform the tasks that bring them great joy and excitement. The bonus to living each day in joy is their ability to make a good living doing so. Once you start to make your desires the dominating theme in your everyday thinking and imagination, your world will start to change.

Not only does your belief in yourself and what you desire to do in life create strong positive emotions, these emotions will also start to dominate your everyday life. Your thoughts will begin to reverberate the theme of your yearning and your impulses on what to do next will start to guide your efforts . You will begin to visualize the ways that your yearning could be accomplished. The more that your focus becomes more defined and specific, the better your subconscious will receive and imprint this new belief in your mind. This begins the momentum toward a desired end rather than to a negative downward spiral. The more fascinating part of this journey is that you will find that you are inclined to take steps in the direction of this calling as your mind begins to adopt that you are what you are called to be in life. You will get urges to take action and call people who will align you with what you desire to be in life. Instead of discussing the scientific and spiritual side of how and why this happens, you only need to know that this will happen and that you will begin to see all areas of your life from a new and higher perspective, where only possibilities exist, and that there is no lack in any area of your life.

You will begin to understand how love and happiness conflict with the ego's plan for blame and excuses. You will come to realize how important and talented you really are in this world and how much love and support there is to help you reach your goals. You need to know that the world is a loving and safe place despite what some of the media and other naysayers want you to know. Knowing all is well is a must to keep you on your path and to raise your children to encounter all the happiness and joy that they can experience. Your children will find this approach to life more natural since most children dream big and follow their impulses to moment-to-moment joy. If not interrupted on this journey, many children would continue to be creative and explore all possibilities of many of their interests in life. The biggest challenge of a family is the parents' ability to allow their children to be who they are called to be instead of crafting them to be something else.

You must desire a better way and raise your standards to achieve a positive state of consciousness and less on what you fear or do not want. This helps to reinforce your new beliefs and brings more positive emotions forward. You need to make compelling arguments to yourself about how moving toward your purpose, health, better relationships, and abundant living will bring you the joy and happiness that you so desire. When you get your beliefs in line with your desires, you will be compelled to act intuitively toward obtaining your desires in life. You will understand that the world is not conspiring against you and that just the opposite is true. You were born to succeed and to be happy and fulfilled. You are on your way to feeling more positive emotions with the anticipation of moving closer to your dreams each day. If you continue to struggle with your demons, you will need to identify exactly what thoughts and beliefs are holding you hostage. Adopting new beliefs can take time, but you always have the choice on whether or not you change your beliefs. If you are not making progress, then you are choosing to hold on to old beliefs. The goal for you is happiness, so if you are not happy, continue to evaluate what thoughts are contributing to your negative emotions.

If you find yourself blaming others or circumstances on your unhappiness, define the exact belief behind the projection of blame. Many of us hold on to the belief that others cause or contribute to our suffering. When you encounter a long-standing and reinforcing belief such as this, challenge yourself by asking a simple question. "Do I have free will?" If you believe that you are free to choose what you think, feel, and act, then you believe that you have free will. If you indeed are given free will, can you honestly believe that someone else can do anything to make you feel, think, or act in a certain way? Even with the logic, we all encounter times when we allow others to influence how we choose to think, feel, and act and differentiate how to divvy up credit and blame. Part of the freedom that you have to choose comes with other beliefs that will be discussed.

The point is not to be too hard on yourself or too defensive. Again, we are human and have flaws. Many people in society have adopted the beliefs that others control their happiness and sadness. The world places a great deal of clout on what others think and little value on self-determination and rugged individualism. You, if like most, are either worried about the future or feel guilty about the past. These are other belief systems that get in the way of progress toward desires and happiness. As you read the remaining chapters in the book, you will be challenged to look at some new truths about life. Do not buy or dismiss any of them too quickly. Take time to fully process each, and look at your beliefs and the new truths, and see which one would lead you in a better direction in life. There are no right or wrong ways or beliefs in the world. There are those that will serve you well; and others, not so well. Again, you have the free will to choose the ones that meet your needs.

Discovering who we are is not an easy process. There are many layers of thoughts and beliefs that constitute our view of the world and the people whom we encounter. Love or fear-related emotions are the results of our thoughts and beliefs. Much of our messages have come from significant others including the media. Our ability to turn off the outside messages is an important first step in analyzing what our internal dialogue is saying about issues such as safety, trust, health, abundance, and our possibilities in life. By shifting our focus to our desires, we can shift from negative emotions to more hopeful feelings. As we allow ourselves to visualize and become excited about our desires, we start to see people and places as more inviting and caring. As we develop our skills to plan our days with thoughts and images of love, peace, and abundance, we begin to discover those activities that bring us the most excitement and joy. As we share our excitement and joy with others, we find ways to use our gifts to serve others. Through our deliberate approach to how we set our new thoughts and beliefs into motion, we come to understand that all is truly well in our world.

Knowing All Is Well

Through your transformation process, you will hope-fully come to the realization that you live in a safe world where you control the outcomes in your life. Your ego has tried and will continue to convince you that bad luck and coincidences are part of your life story when just the opposite is true. Your life is in your control and is playing out based upon your actions that are driven by your conscious and subconscious mind. When you know that the world will respond affirmatively to a positive conscious and subconscious belief system, you will begin to feel free and inspired. When you start to visualize your life purpose with passion and love, you will begin to be inspired to act in ways that will lead you toward the path to what you want and desire. Initially, your wants and desires may begin with the wish for new material possessions. As you move closer to what truly will bring you lasting happiness, you will find that love and harmony with others contains more of the substance you are looking. If you speak to anyone that is in love with life and is truly happy, they will tell you that money and possessions will never bring the true bliss that one's soul's desire will provide. People who let their heart lead their actions know this secret to happiness. The ego will attempt to sell you on the idea that the accumulation of stuff is where the happiness lives.

The great news is as you follow your path to your true purpose and yearning in life, your bank account and your physical health will improve also. When we are following our passions, we experience more joy and less stress, which goes far toward improving overall health and well-being. As for your financial resources, you will soon find out that others will want what you have to offer. Many will pay you well to possess what you are offering if done with passion and service to others. Once you finally lead with your heart and not your ego, you will find that all is really well in your world. You will discover that your former beliefs did not serve any purpose other than to keep you separated from others, your dreams, and from who you really are. You will reach a point where you will gladly help others find out this great secret to happiness, and what better person than your child. The path to happiness is your path to greatness, which will open your eyes to the true beauty and wonder of your world and your child. When you see the world and folks as they truly are, you are ready to share in the true loving relationships that result from positive emotion and expectation.

As you become more and more accustomed to expecting love and harmony in your life, your mind will awaken to a new world, and you will experience life in easier and comforting ways. This may still sound way too good to be true, yet its truth is based upon spiritual, scientific, and psychological principles. The scientific and spiritual laws are becoming more and more prevalent in the thinking today. More doctors, therapists, and scientists are seeing how our thoughts and beliefs do become our reality. If this is the case, the good thoughts must become your new system of beliefs. Most parenting books spend much of the time speaking about interventions and steps to managing developmental barriers. These books do well by guiding parents through how to meet a child's milestones through the developmental stages of life. These resources are beneficial but may lack a proactive approach to parenting that focuses on wellness and well-being as the guiding principles.

Until you are able to manage your thoughts and emotions better, your ability to fully invest your energies to developing your child's best will be quite challenging. You may be able to progress your children through school and even into college and beyond. However, you will not have fully provided a positive thought consciousness to your children that will bring them to the greatest heights and passions to expand to their greatest human potentials. You are your children's mentor and need to impart valuable skills in the area of thought and meeting challenges in life. There is such a poverty of thought that prevails much of society. The thinking of many is "ego-based" fear, which contributes to hurtful, abusive behavior that is seen in families and communities. The irresponsible thinking patterns lead to actions that belittle, humiliate, minimize, abuse, and other emotionally and physically damaging actions. When our first response to any criticism or challenge is to scream, punch, or run away, we are allowing our "fear and lack" outlook in life to control our response to others.

When the concept of poverty is discussed, many believe that the term implies socioeconomic status. For our purposes, the term has more to do with limiting thoughts and beliefs rather than economic resources. When we allow our choices to be highly influenced by others both positively and negatively, we have not chosen a consciousness of abundance where we believe that we can truly chart our course in life. Our course would include a world of infinite possibilities awaiting our decisions. People who think abundantly know that they always find their way through any challenge in life. They possess the ability to see how connected they are with people and places and allow their love and passion to guide them to the possibilities. Those with a poverty consciousness allow fear to guide their decisions and end up taking the path of least resistance. They remain in the same thinking and action patterns that have contributed to their unhappiness. They end up separating themselves from others and their dreams and allow their ego-centered mind to justify why they remain stuck. To bring this back to economics, many people with a poverty thought process would not be able to sustain resources as they would focus on the fear of lack and not be able to sustain the flow of these resources. More stories are being told of the riches-to-rags scenarios. A poverty consciousness repels monetary resources and also relationships.

Your mental health is based upon your ability to neutralize fear and "lack" thinking patterns. You must fully connect the experience your thinking brings to your reality in order to understand just how negative thinking does not make sense or serve you. Too many people are considered mentally ill for thinking thoughts or experiencing a reality based upon fears. They are prescribed medication without being asked to assess their belief systems to fully understand what is causing their fears. There are many people who suffer trauma and other life experiences brought on by their fear. They do not ever make the connection that their lingering challenges are part of their thoughts and beliefs that reinforce their negative experiences in reality. People who hear voices and see images that others do not, have been labeled and heavily medicated instead of being provided the tools to understand that their experiences are based upon their beliefs.

Many practitioners will tell these people that they have false beliefs and/or are hallucinating. The person receiving this information only becomes more fearful as the label of being "crazy" makes them separate more from others and also places their ego in protect mode. The better solution is for the person to realize that their experiences are real to them and are based upon their belief system. The more important issue to address is if the reality experienced is wanted or unwanted. Once a person makes the connection between an unwanted reality and his or her belief system, he or she is on the path to bringing beliefs to the surface for examination and retooling. The subconscious beliefs of a person are very powerful and can do much to ease a person or to make that person feel unease. There are those times when people allow their fears to put them in a state of crisis where the only choice is for services to enact medical responses to protect all involved.

In order for anyone to openly discuss his fears, he must be provided a safe environment to do so without being judged or labeled. So many of our veterans find themselves caught in a belief system that presents them with sounds, smells, visions, and even tactile sensations of the war experience. Without interventions to bring about a change in beliefs, veterans find triggers to their subconscious mind that exacerbate their fears and contributes to their negative feelings and challenges on their return to civilian life. The trauma does not have to remain the dominate belief system if time is spent on honoring the experience and rebuilding a new belief system that serves healing and provides hope. With many parents living with trauma from their past, they would benefit their significant other and children by working on the challenges of their past experiences and building new beliefs that will provide them with a thought process of safety and abundant living while they let go of their thoughts of fear and lack.

You want to see the addition of a child as part of the joy and abundance that you are experiencing. This view allows you to feel blessed and optimistic that you will be guided to more resources to fully meet and exceed the needs of your child. When you are happy and joyful, you gain the natural impulses to nurture your child's mind, body, and soul. You will gain the imagination and playfulness that will match the energy of your child, which is the ingredient for a powerful and meaningful parent-child relationship. Your natural instincts will kick in as you spend each moment of each day in love with your kid. Your emotions of love and joy will expand your thinking and actions to creative endeavors that will provide your child with the stimuli that will fulfill their need to explore, learn, create, and imagine. Your ability to see the infinite possibilities in your life will be passed down to your children as you gain the natural impulses to expose your children to the variety of experiences that will expand their physical, mental, and spiritual capacities.

As part of keeping your thoughts and beliefs moving toward positive and life-fulfilling themes, you will need to change your routine to reflect these new attitudes and beliefs. As mentioned, you need to unplug from the internet and television and, at the very least, restrict your viewing to positive and uplifting experiences that reinforce a positive view of people and the world around you. This will set the stage for your children as they will be most influenced by images that bring about strong emotions. Remember that images and emotions are what the subconscious feeds upon to build your belief system. The more you focus on the joy and great news that is out in the world, the better the outcome for you and your child. As stated, the world and local news bring much emotion and sensationalism to the screen as ratings are necessary for their programs. You want to be informed as to what occurs in your world but not overtaken or consumed by the news and dramas on the media. The statistics show that we live in a safe world and that good news occurs much higher than tragic news. When you consider how many people inhabit the earth and the news that is presented, you can now see that there is a greater positive force keeping the planet peaceful and in harmony.

For your children to move confidently toward life aspirations and purpose, they also must understand that the world is a safe place as this new belief system is paramount to freedom and happiness. Most of the lingering fear and doubt that you may experience will come from the bombardment of negative messages regarding the world, such as scarcity, disease, and death. Your ability to focus on the abundance, health, and positive life moments on this planet will serve you better and will be a great model for others who are caught in the trap of focusing on what they do not want. Before we can start the discussion surrounding how to impart these new approaches with your child, there are some additional barriers to wellness that need to be addressed. These barriers stem from our strong need to be accepted or needed by others, which takes away our personal power and ability to pursue our dreams and desires.

Barriers to Wellness

The first barrier to wellness that you will need to address is the strong emotions brought on by guilt. This emotion is buried in the dark recesses of the subconscious mind as it is fed by the ego in a multitude of ways. You know, all those times you have been rude, cruel, harsh, sarcastic, unloving, absent, abusive, and dishonest with others! Your ego projects these emotions more to cover your feelings of guilt in the form of angry out-bursts or depression born out of your own frustration and pain. You know how well guilt was and is used to get you to perform the way others expect of you. Over the years, your conformity to others' expectations has formed a belief system that you need the approval of others. As you begin to enter adulthood and enter jobs and relationships based upon the expectations of oth-ers, your emptiness turns to negative emotions as you blame others for your unhappiness in life. The ego justi-fies and makes the perfect arguments for allowing your anger and frustration to boil over in hurtful ways as you harbor more and more feelings of guilt. You most likely do not make the association with guilt when you are acting in negative and hurtful ways. Let's take a closer look at what guilt really is to fully make the connection on how this impacts your daily living.

Psychological guilt involves a belief where a deter-mination is made but moral and/or ethical standards were compromised in some way. Since childhood, you were made to believe some of your thoughts and actions were in violation to societal norms, many of which were imposed by others. You may have always dreamed or wanted to pursue a certain career or life purpose and allowed others to talk you out of following your call-ing because you did not want to experience their disap-proval. This occurs in many families as a child is rein-forced to act or believe in what others think is possible and appropriate for them. Many of us learn, at an early, age to allow others to define who we are and continue to do so today.

Guilt contributes to your fear and doubt as you separate more from those dreams and desires that come out from your true yearning. Your feelings of regret that your best days have long passed will ignite fear-based emotions and create beliefs that will contribute to your separation from others. From this guilt, your ego's response is to protect itself resulting in your impulse to attack and blame. The end result is that you will begin to feel less confident, halting your pursuit of your life purpose. Guilt gobbles up your hope and aspirations as you find yourself more absorbed in making arguments for why things do not go your way instead of taking action to improve your life. All one needs to do is listen to the theme of conversations that families and friends engage in. Many discuss their dislikes, which stems from attempts to please others, along with how unfair life is. They resign themselves to "this is the life they were dealt" and gain a sense of martyrdom in their sacrifice to make others happy. In the process of sacrificing, you begin to find that this mentality creates struggle in all areas of your life. Once you adopt a belief that life is a struggle, you will find evidence to support this. You subconscious mind will make this belief a focal point and present the supporting evidence to you each and every day.

Guilt is one of those emotions that *strangles* our psyche. Your attempts to change your thoughts surrounding your regrets is not enough to bring about the positive strong emotions to shift this negative belief system. Many of us feel that we have been harmed in some way by others much more than we have harmed others. The problem with this outlook is that it keeps us stuck, waiting for others to come to us to make peace and resolution. Guilt must be seen as your creation as you have chosen to be bound by it. Your assessment of how you have been treated in life or the justification you have made for hurting others is all your doing. You have placed the negative meaning surrounding what has happened to you. This is not to suggest that you were responsible for the actions of others; rather, a statement to your actions following the incidences that brought you pain. Have you used the occurrences of your past as excuses to treat others poorly or to remain a victim to others? In either case, you have chosen to remain in a belief system that you are unworthy of happiness and that you are a victim of circumstance.

Until people take a leap of faith to making paradigm changes to beliefs and actions to improve their life, this information can be very difficult to understand or even hear. We have been taught that incidences in our lives happen by chance and that we are to be suspicious of others. These concepts alone contribute to our inabilities to remain confident and calm, both of which are needed to be able to remain alert and safe in our life. In either system of beliefs, the best way to become free from the hold of guilt and fear are through the acts of atonement and forgiveness. When you hold no grudges or unresolved conflict with others, you have lifted your own fear that others harbor any ill-feelings or harm against you. The acts of atonement and forgiveness provide a cleansing of your ego-based fear system.

Atonement is a very powerful step in a person's life to right a perceived wrong. More so, the act of atonement brings the emotions of compassion and love to the person making the atonement even if the receiver of the apology rejects the act. This atonement must start with forgiving oneself. Most guilt is self-imposed by a person psychologically directing hurt inward. Guilt is the last glue to the ego's hold on the mind to keep you separate from others and avoid responsibility. As soon as atonement and forgiveness are played out in your life, a miraculous shift occurs where your love and compassion resurfaces as you once felt them prior to the programming of your subconscious with ego themes of doubt, fear, failure, hurt, and other negative messages and images.

There are many ways in which you can atone for acts that have caused you and/or others pain, and to become separated. Some of the people that you need to atone may no longer be living, yet you can still find ways to reconcile with them through spiritual connection. The best way to atone is to find an avenue to communicate your sorrow and love for someone who has been hurt by you, and this avenue must provide the most comfort for the injured person. Some folks may not want to see you in person, so a letter, email, or phone call may be the way to go. Others who want a close relationship with you would prefer a face-to-face encounter. In person, they are able to gain the benefit of accepting your apology and providing you with love. When guilt is lifted from your life, your pursuit of happiness begins to take form in lasting ways. Get into the habit of assessing your interactions with others as to how each made you feel. When your emotions are negative about any interaction, you need to address ways to resolve issues through acts of love and atonement. You may also find that some of your relationships are not serving you well. When others hurt you, you may need to spend less time with them. Moving away from a relationship can also be act of love. The message is not that fear is bad. The message is that you want to make sure that you do not remain fearful and take the steps to bring your emotions in line with love. There will always be people in our lives that we set boundaries. This allows both parties to take part in a unique journey in life that does not impact or judge the other. This assessment helps to identify and restore positive thoughts and emotions while ensuring the ego is managed when it decides to make an appearance on behalf of your fear and frustration.

For those you have wronged but may have already passed away, you can still use visualization and journaling to express atoning sentiments. You can visit their final resting place to connect with them spiritually and present your loving sentiments while asking for forgiveness and knowing that it was granted. Your soul can experience the presence of your deceased love ones when you decide to incorporate this to your belief system. Your ability to connect to your eternalness is crucial in developing a spirituality. One of the contributing factors to all fear is the ego's stance that life ends when the body ceases to function. When we believe that our existence ends in death, we play out life looking for distractions that usually cause harm. Your children need to know that life is eternal in order to understand true joy and happiness. Otherwise, their beliefs will center on the fear that they will eventually disappear. As a parent, you need to find ways to connect to a higher power. There are many resources on spirituality and religion. You owe it to yourself to find those that resonate with you. If you have focused on the messages of this book, the science surrounding the mind and consciousness goes well beyond what can be seen, yet there is enough evidence to show that the mind exists beyond our sensory world. Once you can present images of atonement accompanied by strong loving emotions to your subconscious mind, you will start to resolve the guilt and bring peace to your mind.

The other side to atonement is forgiveness. Your ability to accept an apology is critically important to bringing a relationship to a positive state. If you have problems accepting an apology, you may be harboring some lingering, guilt in your subconscious. Your happiness and joy will be blocked if you do not grant others who seek forgiveness the release from their pain and hurt produced by their guilt. In other words, you do not want to keep others who seek freedom, bound. Of course, this becomes difficult if someone has really hurt you or a family member in a horrific way. You do have the right to choose; however, your choice to forgive not only releases some of the other person's hurt and guilt but also frees you from the anger and hurt that you are harboring toward another human being. Any unresolved negative feelings hinder your journey to happiness and fulfillment. The steps that you take to atone and forgive are the very steps necessary to open your heart to the love that you have repressed. Repressed love and guilt go hand in hand, so your ability to clean up the guilt-laden relationships in your life will go far to your personal growth.

Holding on to grievances and conflict does not contribute to a life of freedom, joy, and happiness. The ego makes very convincing arguments to hold others bound, which cause us hurt, and to place strong judgment on anyone who hurts us. I understand that there are incidences that would be extremely difficult to forgive, yet your willingness to do so will not demonstrate any weakness or lack of love. You ego is driven by fear and is not an accurate assessor of situations, for the act to forgive anyone for any act against you or another person is a true act of love and takes more courage than can be imagined. As a human being and parent, this is one of the greatest lessons to learn and teach. I have written on the act of atonement and forgiveness, and both are needed for healing and love to occur. When you ask for forgiveness or forgive another, you are actually freeing yourself from emotional bondage. All you need to do is to encounter the experience where you forgave or were forgiven. The love that surfaces during this process is powerful and life changing.

The strength gained from the acts of atonement and forgiveness will help catapult you to experience love in the purest forms. When you forgive someone, you will experience the reciprocation of love and also see a transformation of the other person right in front of your eyes. You will truly understand the power of love in this process as you feel the miraculous healing and restoration of peace and harmony in these relationships. To move toward your true calling in life, you must be able to mend as many relationships as possible that cause you angst. You will then be on your way to liberation from the control that you perceive that others have on you. These actions will take away any barriers to the freedom that you are seeking. Later, we will discuss ways to free yourself from the other misperceptions regarding the separation from others and your happiness. Again, you are allowing others to be a barrier to your happiness. You have complete control of how you feel, think, and behave. The key is to convince your mind of this through a belief system that reinforces this.

You can clear your subconscious of guilt and other negative feelings when you bear no ill will toward anyone. You will need to find rituals or thought processes that can get you to a place of peace with others where unresolved issues place you in mental bondage. You really need to address all guilt that you harbor if you are to get on with the pursuit of your happiness. The key to your happiness is to ensure that your mind sees you as the captain of your ship and that your thoughts, feelings, and actions all stem from what you consciously see as your choices. This helps you to make choices you can live with, the understanding that you are responsible for the results and no one else. This freedom will provide you with the starting point in your transformation to the person that you want to be and truly are. Guilt and other negative emotions distract you from experiencing the present moment. You end up worrying about the future or regretting the past. To live in the moment and enjoy what life offers presently, you need to focus your attention away from past and future thoughts that reinforce many of the negative emotions that you experience. As the focus of the book shifts to raising your children, you will see how important living in the present is. You will also gain a better understanding of the development of your children as you remain focused on their development and creativity. The trick is to understand that your worries and doubts serve no purpose in your life. You know this to be true, yet your day can be consumed with both rather than enjoying what you experience moment by moment. Negative emotions will keep you from progressing emotionally, socially, spiritually, and physically in life. True happiness is dependent upon your ability to expand to higher fulfillment and contribution to the world. Anyone who is stuck in neutral will become bored and lifeless.

If you look at the famous people who seem to possess everything from fame to riches, you will find that many are depressed and extremely unhappy because their lives are not expanding to positively impact the world. They have allowed others to define who they are and have attempted to fit into a lifestyle that focuses on the superficial rather than love for others and life. Happiness is and always will be found when you act on your highest passion and joy, which will expand as you focus more on your gifts and talents. Your excitement and joy will come from your service to others by your talents rather than from material wealth or fame you receive from your services. You were born to express your true being to the world as only you can. Until you allow yourself to do what you were born to do, you will not feel fulfilled and experience sustained joy and happiness. With this understanding, you see the importance of providing a home environment for your children where they can express and create at their highest joy without adopting negative belief patterns that have hindered you.

Coming to a conclusion that all is well in life takes some restructuring to our thinking patterns and beliefs. Our thoughts are greatly influenced by significant others. Through our years, we encounter people that we have hurt and who have hurt us. Many times, the issues surrounding the hurt are never resolved and remain a looming presence in our subconscious minds. The emotions that surface from unsolved hurt and pain from relationships are guilt and fear. You may find yourself expressing other negative emotions such as anger and frustration during your day or you may be depressed. The acts of atonement and forgiveness go far to dissolving the negative emotions that stem from the hurt and pain of relationships. To gain the ability to focus on happier thoughts and directions in life, you must atone and forgive others to release guilt and fear from your subconscious. By doing so, you will be better equipped to focus on the present moment. Happiness only exists in the present moment, and many people seldom remain present for any sustained time frame. When you resolve issues with others, you become better able to focus on the present since worry and guilt are kept in check. Children naturally remain present, which frustrates some parents as they need time to worry and stress or to completely distract from reality. The only way to help your children find their purpose is for you to become present with them.

Helping Your Child Grow and Find Their Life Purpose

You must want to know what this book has to do with parenting. You just went through an internal assessment of your current and past beliefs and thinking, in which need retooling. I will let you in on a secret that will help you in all areas of your life. You will not see success in your roles as parent, intimate partner, friend, or coworker, or experience good health and abundant living, unless you gain control of your thoughts and develop positive and uplifting beliefs and attitudes. Once you have accomplished a new consciousness that sees life as exciting, joyful, and happy, you will act in ways that will support and nurture this view. You have most likely been told that the decision to have a child is not to be taken likely. By now, you know why and are better prepared to take the exciting journey of parenthood, which starts out miraculously and will continue that way as long as you remain in a positive consciousness. Get ready for a great adventure as your child will provide the environment that reveals the change, certainty, connection, and relevance that you need in life.

How well your journey goes is based upon your ability to grow and to contribute beyond your own needs.

There are plenty of books that describe prenatal and infant care from a medical standpoint. Your ability to nurture the spiritual, physical, social, intellectual, and emotional well-being of your children is critical, especially during the first five to seven years of their lives when their minds and bodies are developing at great speed. Much of your children's subconscious beliefs are entrenched by age seven. You control much of what you allow your children to be exposed. The result of this exposure can be observed in your children's physical and/or emotional development at very early ages. Since the subconscious mind records all that is presented to it as truth right from the start of life, you want to be sure that your infant is spoken to in loving sentiments that provide the types of messages that support safety, love, trust, fun, laughter, and other happy tones. Having an infant that cries through the day and night can test parents or caretakers. As difficult as this may sound, your facial expressions, words, and sounds are being recorded by your child, which can negatively impact them during their early development.

During the first year of life, a child's needs extend beyond food, diapers, and medical appointments. An infant needs to feel you close and hear your voice. They need to stretch out beyond a crib or playpen and be exposed to pictures in books, songs, and media that may help them see many beautiful and spectacular images and sounds of love, adventure, and happiness. If you are letting others spend time with your child, you will want to ensure that these same types of messages and needs are met. The most important contribution that you can make to your child at the earliest of stages is to grow their excitement of books by reading to them as much as you can and showing them books with fun and exciting pictures. These pictures should include images of nature along with people, animals, and places that are filled with bright colors and fun themes. The books should carry virtuous tones and themes that demonstrate love, respect, honesty, and other positive attributes as you are building the positive attitudes and beliefs that correspond with healthy and loving people.

There are many parents and caretakers who send their children to daycare centers. These parents may become very uncomfortable reading this as other caretakers are nurturing your child. My response to those who send or will send their child to daycare is to do what you feel is most right for you and your child. Ask yourself if you are happy with your decision. If you are not, what are your other options? You may not have any other options, so you will need to make sure that the time you do spend with your child encompasses what is being outlined. As stated, your children's beliefs and needs can be met if you become the most significant person in their lives. Make every moment count with your child as each moment and action on your part contributes to their development. Make sure to screen everyone who watches your child to ensure that they carry out your itinerary to ensure physical, social, emotional, intellectual, and spiritual needs are fostered and nurtured.

The time that you spend with your child will be critical for the next five to six years of development. Be sure to expose them to music, books, recreation, culture, and spiritual practices. Your involvement must be at a high level where you are exposing your child to many sensory experiences and learning. From this, you will develop their intellect, physical agility skills, and their ability to dream, think, and create from feelings of joy, happiness, and excitement. You also will become of great significance to your child as your ability to share in their journey of wonderment will forever place you as part of their joyful and loving experiences at the most crucial part of their development. Your investment of time will begin to pay out dividends far beyond what you can fathom as you become the most significant person in your child's life and the one that matters to him/her most. When friends, acquaintances, and/or entertainment sources are more significant than parents, then the parent-child struggles begin to mount. The more time invested in your children from birth on, the easier the child management in later years.

You can set the stage where books, numbers, recreation, music, and art have meaning and learning is highly regarded. Playing games is a great part of learning and recreating but should be done as a board game, not a computer game, especially in the early stages of development. The computer is a great tool, but a child's development is better served interacting side by side with real people at a slow pace. Television and computers have activities for kids who run at fast speeds and may get many kids overstimulated and anxious.

As a parent or caretaker, you must monitor your child's activities to ensure that they are developing the skills necessary to read social cues and react accordingly. Emotional intelligence is just as critical as mental intelligence as many careers are never started or lost due to a person's inability to react appropriately to others in a workplace. By interacting face-to-face, you are helping your child learn social skills of reciprocal play and parallel play. Children who receive individual attention from parents can participate in solo and multiple child activities in age-appropriate ways and do not experience the need to disrupt or be the center of attention.

To ensure that your child is active and learning how to think and process information, you must get off your computer and tell your Facebook friends that you have better things to do. Your own distractions will keep you from your child along with your own pursuits of your life purpose. On your path to your personal dreams and calling in life, you will gain valuable skills by properly developing your child as this is a very important part of your journey. No matter what you are called to do on earth, raising your child is an integral part of this calling. Introduce yourself to your inner child and enjoy the fun and activities by being actively involved in reading books, singing songs, playing kickball, drawing pictures, and much more. After your children reach the age of seven, you will begin to see them become more selective in what they like, and this is where the real fun begins. If you play, read, run, jump, throw, catch, draw, visit museums, and attend other cultural and spiritual events with your child, you may also find some stuff you prefer. You and your child just may discover what your souls have called you both to do through your effective parenting. Now it is time to nurture and progress you and your child through the journey of your lives.

Get Moving

During this time, are you finding yourself enjoying time with your child, or are you gravitating toward old habits. These old routines may consist of placing your kid in front of a television while you spend hours on the computer? In addition to developing thoughts and beliefs that align with happiness and love, you will want to take crucial steps toward building a mind-body connection. When our thoughts continue to teeter back and forth between positive and negative themes, the one critical action that one must take is to strengthen the body. Not only is this critical for your physical health, but it is also critical for your emotional health. When you can start pushing your physical body to become more in line with what you want, then you will begin to link your body and mind, where you make more associations with well-being. The mind-body connection is crucial for any long-term success path in your life. Exercise will increase your vitality and energy and bring your emotions back to a more positive state of well-being. Your body may need to take progressive steps, but there are numerous options for exercise based upon your present physical state and your physician's recommendations. The brain will start to produce some chemicals that will help progress your ability to adopt more positive thoughts and beliefs as well-being from exercise opens the gateway to seeing possibilities and more hope.

When you become more physically fit from exercise, you will also be better equipped to engage your child in physical activities, which will further enhance your relationship, and this may also allow you to be a role model to benefit your child's physical activity. Your children will benefit by playing outdoors and understanding how good they will feel from running around and engaging in physical recreation. The hardest part to exercise is to make the decision to start moving. By just walking in nature, you will instantly feel the benefits of moving your body and experiencing nature. Physical activities also help to bring about spirituality, which is an important ingredient to your journey in life. Do not confuse spirituality with religion as spirituality is more of your personal journey and connection to people, nature, and your higher power in the manner that speaks to you. Finding your peace and harmony in life through your choice of beliefs that bring you happiness and love is a spiritual experience that is not based on a religious denomination. You do not need to abandon your religious beliefs in this process of adopting a personal spirituality. You and your children will enjoy life with the knowing of spiritual connection in the manner that makes the most sense to each of you.

By the time your children enter school, they will have demonstrated particular skills and abilities that are more pronounced than others. At this stage in their development, you want to continue to expose your children to a wide variety of recreational, educational, and social activities that can promote their creativity, resulting in the formulation of interests and desires. Spend time each day observing what your children do to entertain or stimulate themselves when alone. Ask your children about their preferences and what activities bring out their joy and happiness. Try not to judge their answers or discourage their desires or interests. Your children are at a very creative and imaginative stage where all possibilities are on the table. Remember, their belief system continues to be developed, which absorbs messages from all those they encounter. These encounters can create positive and negative experiences for your children that impact their well-being. Do not shelter your children from conflict or the world. As your children remain confident and happy, they will respond to challenges better. Children must learn how to manage and solve conflict as this skill will be of great value throughout their lives. You want to ensure that your children communicate issues surrounding conflict with you. Your ability to instill beliefs that support love is critical. Teaching your children to understand their worth is not based upon others' opinion is very critical to their happiness. Children at the earliest years in school will attempt to influence your children's self-esteem and self-worth. When you can teach them to love and respect children without allowing others' views to persuade theirs, you will have imparted the most empowering belief regarding relationships. The more confident and happy your children are, the less they will encounter conflict in their lives as their emotional intelligence will help them to attract children who think and behave in the same manner. The children looking to bully others look toward the children who are more vulnerable and less confident.

The most fundamental act of love that parents or caretakers can do for their child is to spend time teaching their child to read, write, add, subtract, multiply, and divide. When you read, sing, and count with your child, you bring fun to education and help your child master these skills. As stated, uncertainty is a need in our lives or life would become monotonous, yet children also need to possess certainty through mastery of the basic skills in which all subjects in school progress. Parenting with love and purpose is taking time from your own downtime to spend an hour or two each night reviewing mathematic flash cards and reading together. Mastery in these basic areas provides the certainty needed for your child to find education less frightening and more of a positive life experience. Your child needs to develop a belief system that acknowledges the importance of learning and also to embrace change or uncertainty as a process for gaining new knowledge and skills. Many parents share their belief that school can be a waste of time and that public school does not adequately teach. Your children will quickly adopt your beliefs, so make them positive and productive.

There are additional ways to enhance your child's experiences and to ensure that his or her talents are recognized and have progressed. These include exposing your child to social, recreational, cultural, educational, and other activities that may help your creative and expressive child connect with images, sounds, smells, and tastes of some of what is possible in life. Many times, this exposure can only be accomplished through viewing magazines, movies, and other media when you have limited resources where you live. The point is to allow your child to witness some of the sounds, physical sensations, smells, pictures, and tastes in life and to monitor which ones make an impression. You must take hold and become one of your children's interests where you help to bring out these abilities and following through to ensure they engage more in certain preferred activity themes. As a parent, you will want to recognize these talents and interests and help your child connect to activities and events that progress these skills, later helping him/her to connect his/her talents to future careers.

For example, a child who loves to draw and look at pictures can be exposed to different types of art or even architectural models. The point is to expose your children to as many variations of their interests and talents as possible to allow them to make choices, or even try multiple options to see which matches their abilities and desires better. Some children show interests and abilities in a multitude of disciplines, which all need to be explored as best as possible. Any aptitude has limitless possibilities, so do not burden yourself with having to know what steps to take in the progression. Just allow your child to experience as much as possible through books and activities, and their path will begin to surface. As long as you stay in tune with your children, they will begin to communicate their likes and dislikes and share what they want to explore.

A critical skill to develop during your children's exploration into the various paths of possibilities is their ability to consciously think about experiences from the highest vantage points, which are happiness, excitement, and joy. This is why your ability to transform your thinking prior to raising your child is very critical. While your children are developing beliefs that make up their consciousness, you want to introduce several truths about life to them. These truths will help them to reach higher creative and intellectual abilities while supporting positive attributes of hope, joy, excitement, freedom, love, kindness, and compassion. These truths are ones that will help you and your child reach emotional, social, physical, and spiritual well-being in life. From this well-being, you and your child will experience positive relationships, more abundance, better health, and the life purpose you always yearned to have.

The first truth is that people can be trusted. The conscious thought and subconscious belief that others can be trusted is critical if your child is ever going to experience joy and love in life. Knowing that the world is safe and inhabited by trustworthy people makes this become more of a reality for your child. The ego will be reluctant to agree as the ego loves to show evidence of violence and untrustworthy people out in the world. So many people share the belief that the world is coming to a final end and never really find hope and peace in their hearts. As difficult as this may be to believe, your beliefs and thoughts become what you experience and perceive in life. To fear and doubt people in your life will only bring about betrayal and other negative outcomes. You and your child's ability to gain a trust consciousness will enable each of you to act in ways that will attract and bring out the best in others around you. Your children's ability to know that people can be counted on to lend a hand or provide bridges to the gaps in life will help them find peace of mind and a true belief in their ability to achieve anything they desire.

The belief that their world is safe and filled with loving and compassionate folks will enhance your child's need for connection and love and will reinforce their conscious efforts to love others. There are really just two emotions that guide all positive and negative emotions. These are the emotions of fear and love. The ego drives fear as the vehicle to keep you separated from others and is filled with anxiety, worry, doubt, stress, and other debilitating feelings. Your child's ability to love is the true belief that they knew prior to any programming. Your ability to mentor and reinforce acts of love and compassion to others will help your child pursue the best path in life to meet their developmental milestones. You will have many opportunities to reinforce this belief with your children as they are exposed to many different types of people, places, and activities. From love, their passion for life will grow, and their true calling will present itself during their growth and development.

The next truth is that all human beings are worthy to want and receive all good that comes their way. As you are learning, the way you view your own worth plays out in how you perceive others. As we blame others or make excuses for why we do not have what we think we want in life, the more we are saying that we do not feel worthy of the things that we want. Many times, we are what we perceive and label in others. This may be a hard truth for an adult; however, children do not come into the world judging others or disliking who they are. Many kids are happy to see others and gladly accept others no matter how they look, smell, talk, or even act. They learn to discount their worth as messages are powerfully delivered by significant adults and peers who bring new beliefs about their worth and success. Many of these significant people share their biases and judgments toward others. The truth that all people are worthy of love is a message that escapes many in society that separate people into groups, categories, and other compartments in order to label and make judgment to their worthiness of love.

The best gift that you can bestow on your child is the gift of knowing their worth is not contingent upon the approval of others. Since we all live in a world that does separate and judge, your child's ability to live life independent of the approval of others is most significant to their sustained joy and happiness. This includes your approval. As a parent, you must be able to separate a child's behavior from their worth. This may be very difficult for you as you were most likely made to believe that your actions somehow determine your worth as a human being. As long as you hold on to this belief and bestow this on your child, you will both be controlled by the labels that others place on you, which will force both of you to act in ways that do not adhere to your true identity, only to that identity that you think others want. This point cannot be stressed enough for most worry and depression stems from how persons gain acceptance to be who they truly think others want them to be.

Guilt, which was discussed earlier, is enacted by making your worth contingent upon others and is very crippling to living life with emotional freedom. At early ages, a child is told that a certain behavior is necessary to gain the love and affection of a parent. How a child dresses, talks, eats, plays, and sleeps is critiqued by parents and many times connected to how love is expressed or withheld by parents. Helping your child to adopt acceptable manners, dress, and social graces is a role that you play. The important distinction is how you play your role. You can remain loving and kind to your child even when he or she does not conform to your standards. She may take some time to learn social norms and values that bring her in line with social norms that are acceptable. Your children can understand there are options on how to behave to help make it easier for them to make friends, show responsibility, and other expectations without connecting her abilities to self-worth. Your love for your children or their self-worth should not be contingent on any action on their part.

Your ego may disagree and exclaim that kids who do not listen and break rules need to be punished and taught lessons in life. You may think that your child needs to show respect to get respect and also needs to consider your feelings if they want your love. Your ego will make the case that your children's every action should be in line with what you expect, need, and want from them. Your parents treated you this way, and you turned out okay. Did you really? If you worry about what others think, then you did not turn out free to be your own person and to take the risks to make you truly happy. Your child will always need your guidance and direction while knowing that your love is ever present in the process. When did parenting become an adult-child battleground? In many cases, the children deemed the most problematic in a family were the ones who actually attempted to demonstrate their worth by holding their ground on what they believed and wanted. Society has made the case that conformity is the road to civility when in fact this is not the truth. There were ruthless leaders in the history of mankind who killed many citizens while staying within the rules of the society. The most revered pioneers of history broke the rules and challenged the status quo. There is a difference from breaking the rules and breaking laws. This is not to condone breaking laws. This is to point out that the true happy people did not come out of conventional thought or practices.

Education and other community institutions will demand your child to conform and will also promote what they term as "high self-esteem." The problem occurring today with the self-esteem drive is that institutions are pushing messages that inflate a child's esteem beyond the child's true abilities. For example, the message is that kids are performing well and that everyone wins and passes class without actually demonstrating the skills, which only inflates the ego in artificial ways. There are more statistics showing the increase of narcissism in children, which only creates the emptiness that comes from the realization that their abilities and skills needed to accomplish goals are not present. Once children or any person that possess an inflated ego system discover that they do not possess the attributes needed in the given area, they will act in ways to remain elevated at the expense of others. Their fear of being discovered as frauds makes them act in ways that keeps their ego inflated while laying a path of hurtful and destructive behavior. You may have worked for this kind of person, one who supervises others but lacks the skills to truly perform the duties of the job. This person will deflect blame and responsibility when goals are not met and will take credit for others' accomplishments.

The rise in bullying in schools is not an issue of low self-esteem as presented by the schools. More and more cases of bullying are shown to be by children of any socioeconomic status and ethnicity. More so-called popular kids are bullying children who present themselves in unique and creative ways. Kids who are different from the norm are the victims of the bullying in many cases. The bully needs to feed their inflated esteem by controlling and overpowering others. Parents and institutions have failed to understand compassionate approaches to child development, which include kindness and love while helping children develop their true talents and abilities. This is what reinforces self-worth and helps children remain grounded in the reality of their actual skill levels. With this same compassion and love, parents and other professionals can help children to understand that any weak areas can be strengthened through skill development, which means more work and effort. As a parent, you never want to give your children false praise or accolades when they really do not show an aptitude or skill in an area of life. This does not mean that you cannot encourage them to work hard to develop the skill and show them the compassion that goes with positive and constructive feedback. Praising children for putting forth a great effort is different from providing a false acknowledgement that they demonstrate a particular skill set. Children need encouraged and celebrated with honest and loving messages.

What can ease your child's worry and doubt about not showing proficiency in certain areas? The answer surrounds the next truth; there really is no competition for the resources and opportunities in the world due to the infinite possibilities and endless abundance. Wars have been fought, ulcers developed, and worry and doubt magnified over the false belief that scarcity and limited resources are present in the world. The whole competition for positions and places in the world only drives stress and worry, which contribute to the neuroses of children. The belief of scarcity becomes a reality as possibilities are diminished by feelings of fear, doubt, and hopelessness. Your child needs to see the world as abundant. Nature demonstrates this each day as the earth produces yields from plant, animal, and elements that sustain life in an abundant way. The distinguishing factor of this truth is the concept of living life from the inside out. What this implies is that our internal thoughts and beliefs must be nourished with messages that reinforce our creative genius where each of us possesses an abundance of choices and possibilities to impact the world with our gifts and talents.

Your children need to know that their abilities and internal resources will ensure abundance in life no matter what the condition of the economy and the amount of people on the planet. As your children connect to the conscious belief that they are living in abundance and have the ability to possess what they want, they will be inspired to act in ways that will move them in the direction of their desires. When fear, worry, and doubt are absent in children who grasp the concept of unlimited possibilities, their natural tendency to dream and create will continue to move them toward their passions. The fearless in life are people who possess great abundance throughout the world.

Another truth your children need to embrace is that they control the outcomes in their lives. This truth entails that life is not happenstance and circumstances are not coincidences. All consequences of life are connected to the thoughts and belief systems that are dominant in their subconscious minds. Even the things not wanted in life begin to show up when the thoughts are dominant in one's thinking. There are spiritual, scientific, and psychological evidence to back this, which is becoming more publicized as time goes on and more studies show how people do indeed attract people, events, and circumstances that match their thinking and feeling patterns. What does this mean? For our purpose, this means that you create your reality—the good, bad, and ugly in life. Once you and your child accept this truth, you will be liberated from victimhood in this world. This is not to imply that you deserve bad things to occur in your life.

As a parent, being a role model for the kind of thinking and beliefs that do not limit or excuse life circumstances will provide a positive environment for your child to connect to their true being, one that is filled with happiness and love. You will need to resist your urges to step in and restrict choices and make your child feel guilty for not adhering to your needs. You are responsible for teaching your child, yet you are not suppose to place shame, blame, or guilt on your child for their wanting to express some self-reliance. You want to place structure and rules that help your child remain safe and supported to develop and learn positive social norms, values, and virtues. When you start to control your children's journey even though they are not imposing on the structure and values of the home, you are creating resistance that will only lead to your children's frustration and anger.

The parental dance is easier if the parent has the conscious mind of love, which stems from the understanding and beliefs in the system outlined. If you are broken and wounded, your ability to help your child reach a state of happiness and joy is very limited You will experience much difficulty seeing your child as a unique, creative, and unlimited being. Instead, you will focus more on those behaviors and characteristics that you feel justify your frustration and anger, which will victimize your child's development. This will feed the ego of your child, and enact an ego response of separation in your relationship. This feeling of separateness will further alienate your child from thinking and feeling that the world is a safe place and will reinforce your view of the world as unsafe and cruel.

Your children's reliance on you for their basic needs make them learn early that they must yield to your way of thinking and feeling. Even though this is a choice they make, there really is limited choosing when a child's experience to the world is limited. This is why a parent's role is so critical and important to understand. You must monitor and maintain your emotional well-being to ensure that you provide the positive environment necessary for your child's nurturing. When you act in any manner that involves negative emotions, you are attacking the emotional system of a child who is not born to understand your angry outbursts and menacing nonverbal communication.

The next truth focuses on the concept of stress. Stress is not real. Simply asked, can you touch, taste, smell, or see the concept of stress? Certainly you feel stress and see people who claim to be under stress. The fact is that stress is engineered by our own faulty thought processes. Stress is a concept that came about when human beings gave away their internal control to external factors. The biggest external factor that provides most of our stress is the expectations of other people. Simply put, we care about what others think and say about us. We really believe we need others to approve of us and go to extremes for this approval. You will teach your child to do the same if you are not careful. Our society is filled with people pleasers. What can possibly be wrong with pleasing others? Nothing and everything!

If pleasing someone is the result of you performing in ways to meet your goals and dreams, you are more likely to appreciate the recognition. If pleasing someone has caused you to abandon your principles and desires in life, you are relinquishing your power, resulting in fear, worry, and stress. You are also allowing your beliefs to drift to a view of losing your control, losing your freedom and joy in the process. Stress comes from all negative emotions that surface when you compromise who you are and what you yearn to be. This discussion sounds very similar, doesn't it? All roads lead to the same place. You are either heading to your soul's desire or you are suffering stress. The same will be said of your children if they do not understand that their self-reliance is the road to happiness. Self-approval is the only approval of any substance. In the event that others also approve, the sweeter it will be! The key is to not seek approval as your motivation to perform in certain ways.

Previously, you were introduced to your ego and ways that fear shows up as guilt and worry. When your children are controlled externally, they are also caught up in anticipating future outcomes or reviewing past issues. In either case, stress is summoned when worry, doubt, guilt, and fear become the reality in which one cares what others think regarding decisions and actions. You may wonder how examples of stress can be shown when a truth that there is no stress, is touted. The key point made is that stress is manufactured by our minds from a choice in how one chooses to perceive at a given situation. Teaching your child to remain in the present moment helps to keep them free from the feelings of worry and guilt. There is only a continuous "now," experience in life. The present moment is the only real moment in you and your children's lives. The sooner you figure that out, the sooner you can join your child in having incredible fun and joy in each of these "now" moments throughout the day and the rest of your lives.

In order to keep your feelings of guilt and doubt in check throughout your life, you must learn the importance of selfishness. Selfishness is different from arrogance and apart from the way your ego separates you from others. Selfishness entails taking care of your physical, mental, social, and spiritual needs. When your needs are nurtured and fed, you are better equipped to engage people and allow them to act in ways without triggering negative thoughts and emotions. Through your selfishness, you want to consume all the knowledge and resources to enhance the person you are and will become in important areas of your life. This helps you develop the self-love needed to embrace others more fully and to be a beacon of hope for others to find their happiness. You will be better able to manage the negativity of others without leaving your position of well-being when you love yourself. Instead of feeling the pain of others, you will invite them to share in your joy. The world has placed a negative connotation to selfishness. To take care of and love yourself must be a first step in your journey if you are to be a parent that can express love to your child. Too many parents believe that they must sacrifice for their families. They deny their needs for well-being and experience problems in their relationships, finances, health, and spirituality. When you believe that you must sacrifice, your reality becomes one of sacrifice.

Once you and your child embrace that you are in control of what you choose to think and feel, you can begin to understand that negative emotions are a choice. You choose to think negatively when you allow yourself to look to the past and future and make the decision to give your power to others. When you perceive others to have power over you, your ego will enact thoughts that result in blame, shame, fear, self-loathing, procrastination, and other negative thinking patterns. You and your child will grow developmentally by understanding that all things are possible and that self-reliance is the key to your happiness. You are the captain of your ship, and you can choose to allow your thoughts, feelings, and actions to be inspired by your authentic wants and desires. People who experience true happiness accept full responsibility for their lives, which includes each and every decision and outcome that comes their way. They see setbacks as learning experiences and enjoy the journey as much as or more than the arrival to their destination. You will want your children to discover that they possess all the internal fortitude to create and live the life that they want. In the end, this leads to the truth that reinforces all truths.

The truth be known, you and your child do not want to be told what to do. As simple and easy as this truth sounds, many folks also love to tell people what to do! Your children do need structure, and there are times you will need to direct their activities. The foundation of this truth is that people, including you and your children, like to be provided choices and allowed to make decisions independently when possible. Children develop best when they gain mastery in each of their developmental stages. This mastery only comes when they are allowed to act and try the skills in that stage of development. There are times when children can get to the same mastery level through creative means. Your child needs to be allowed to form their creative decision making to reach mastery in skills as conformity is not a natural desire for children. Allowing children to be "rebels" or "mavericks" is great if they do not hurt others or impose on other's rights. You will find that the great innovators and life changers of the world did not follow convention. When you look at the level of distractions and addictions that are present in the world, you are witnessing the outcomes to people who did not exercise their right to choose the life. Many people who have based their life journey on others opinions and views feel empty and spend their days consumed with worries while repressing their creativity and imagination.

You Can't Do That

Parents face the challenge of either allowing their children to grow or telling them how to think, feel, and act. Many parents teach their child by pointing out what that cannot do. They wait to catch their children "screwing up" rather than demonstrating patience. Patience includes providing choices and allowing children to chose their preferred response. Allowing your children to explore and solve issues is part of their development. Parents also discourage their children from attempting difficult tasks or challenges. Many forbid their kids to attempt certain tasks; exclaiming that the task is beyond their ability. As long as the child's safety is not at risk, allow your child to attempt challenging tasks that engage their positive and critical thinking. There are studies that show how pessimists do much better than optimists in standardize tests. Many optimists overstate their abilities to understand complex issues, but this does not tell the story of life success. The same groups were also researched on success. The optimists achieved much higher than the pessimists for they were more willing to take risks.

As a parent, you most certainly can teach social, physical, and academic skills to your children throughout their development. Your parental role centers on involving your child in a multitude of activities. You want to spend time together in physical play, mental games, social engagement, ethnic and multicultural experiences, art, music, and exposure to other community, state, country, and world treasures. The sky is the limit as your child's brain has the ability to absorb more data than any supercomputer. Books are the one medium that can bring much exposure to your child. Once you get your child valuing books, you have set in motion one of the truths that will catapult your child ahead of others and make your life as a parent much easier. The truth is that seeking knowledge and information expands knowledge and possibilities, which keeps our soul alive and well. If you are not expanding as a person, you are dying. You and your children's purpose in life, is to expand to what you truly yearn to be. If you can say that you are content in life, then you have found the path to what brings out your true passions and talents. The more exposure your children receive to the possibilities in life, the better chance that they will resonate with one or more interest that call to them.

Your children will appreciate the exposure to a variety of activities and subject themes, so you want to bring these activities and themes to life through books and reading. Make reading become as exciting to them as playing games on the computer. Children who love books and reading are the best achievers in school as everything in school curriculum is based on their ability to read and comprehend the written word. Your ability to involve your child in connecting to books will pay you dividends as your child embraces the school experience much easier than those who find reading mundane or difficult. The key for parents is to be involved in the initial stages of introducing their children to books. Reading to your child and sharing the pictures with excited emotion goes far to get your child's subconscious mind to believe that books are fun and stimulating. Your efforts to read to and with your child will bring words to images in their mind, which will stimulate their resourcefulness and help them to develop the skills to dream and imagine.

Your need to expand your life experiences is also very great, so you can also build upon your interests with your child and discover stimulating people, places, and information that can help you transform to the person you were meant to be. Your transformation is really about finding out who you are but have been talked out of or felt unworthy to be. When you expose yourself to more life experiences, you will realize some of your childhood dreams can become your reality. Many people think that they need a plan of action to find what they are looking for. Just the opposite is true. You only need desire and the willingness to break from your routine to try new adventures to get this ball rolling. Adults tend to overthink everything and end up paralyzing their efforts as the end desire seems way too difficult. Details will come later as you take time to explore new paths in life. So goes the path of your children! Your children will begin to dream about what they want to be in life way before the "how tos" ever surface, yet all the great innovators saw the dream from the end game before being inspired to move in the direction of the achievement.

Developmental Outcomes for Children

When you and your child are engaged in many different activities, you can gauge your child's progress by ensuring the following skills are developing prior to entering school:

Jay Krunszyinsky

- **Gross motor:** using large groups of muscles to sit, stand, walk, run, etc., keeping balance, and changing body positions.
- **Fine motor:** using hands to be able to eat, draw, cut with scissors, dress, play, write, and do many other things.
- **Language:** speaking and annunciating clearly, using body language and gestures appropriately, and understanding and responding appropriately to what others say.
- **Cognitive:** thinking creatively, processing information accurately evidenced by learning ability, understanding information, problem-solving, reasoning, and remembering.
- **Social:** initiating interactions with others, having relationships with family, friends, and teachers, cooperating, and responding appropriately to the feelings of others.

Your children will develop these skills as you and others engage them in educational, physical, and social activities. The more time that you spend with your children immersed in fun and play, the better developed they will become. Your children will match your enthusiasm or lack thereof, so your ability to see the world from a child's perspective is very critical to your effectiveness as a parent. This is why so much of the focus was spent on your ability to return to love and happiness. Once you become aligned with your true self and your soul's desire, you will find your inner child expand

and begin to drive you towards seeing the world with the wonderment you once possessed.

By age five, your children will begin to develop language, cognitive, and physical skills that will enable them to enter school with the ability to engage teachers and students at the level of development needed to continue making developmental progress. Some of the skills your child would possess at this point would consist of but not limited to the following:

Language

During the time spent reading stories to your children and engaging them in games and other social activities, they will begin to demonstrate the ability to recall stories and speak in sentences of more than a few words. Your children will be able to express some emotions and tell their own stories of events in their lives. Your children will be able to recite a number sequence and recite the alphabet. Having number and alphabet books is a great way to introduce your children to these basics.

Cognitive Milestones

Your ability to acclimate your children to a schedule of activities each day helps bring a routine and the concept of time to their lives. Your children will begin to distinguish differences in objects and know the basic shapes and size differences. He will also be able to understand the different types of furniture and appliances in the home. As a parent, you can introduce your children to much more thought provoking activities such as puzzles, memory games, and object finding activities. Prior to entering school, you want to introduce your children to basic reasoning and problem-solving skills that focus on their ability to identify basic acts of right and wrong, which can be found in many books on virtues for children. Teaching your children to take responsibility for hurtful acts towards others is an important developmental skill. Atonement processes involving an apology and acts of love will help your children to express love rather than anger and frustration. As a parent, you must role model the same behavior to your children. Take the time to take responsibility for when you demonstrated negative emotions. Making apologies and atoning for hurtful behavior needs to be reciprocated by you and will go far to keeping you significant and credible to your child.

Social

There are some basic skills necessary for your child to engage other children upon entering school. One of these skills is his ability to play cooperatively with others. You can assist your child to develop this skill during those times that you are engaged in games and other fun activities. Demonstrate cooperation in the form of taking turns when it comes to conversing and playing games. The more attention that your children receive the better they will be able to manage their need for attention. In other words, many children that are starved for attention tend to dominate conversations and play. Engaged children are at peace with you and the world and begin to mirror your social presentation. Your children should also be able to play solo without disturbing others that play parallel to them. Again, you are a key person in the modeling of this with your children as you provide activities in which your children can engage individually while you work on your passion and hobby next to them. Parallel play and cooperative play skills are very critical skills that are modeled and reinforced through your ability to remain involved and engaged with your children throughout the early years of development.

As mentioned, your children need to develop their sense of right and wrong, as well as, to follow basic rules of conduct in a structured setting. As a parent, you can begin to teach these skills in social settings. Take your children to the local museum, library, church, and other local community resources that require basic rules for attendance. Your children will learn to follow rules regarding when to speak, what to touch, and how to delay wants and gratification. By participating in church or other spiritual settings, you and your children can review basic moral tenants where your children begin to formulate the concepts of love, respect, and honesty. Spirituality and religion are critical for development and hope needed for children to remain in love and a mindset of infinite possibilities in life. This is also true for you!

Physical Development

Playing outside and at recreational centers with your children will do wonders to develop their gross motor skills. You will also find that you will benefit from the fresh air and exercise as these activities go far in improving emotion and overall health. During physical play, you can teach your children to skip, jump and run. Playing tag has and always will be the most welcomed activity of a child for it brings pure exhilaration. I dare you to find an unhappy child when being chased in a game of tag. Physical play can also consist of some pitch and catch activities but with light, soft and squishy balls tossed at close proximities. These skills continue to develop as children enter school and progress towards preadolescence.

Physical play can also include dancing, singing, and play acting. Your ability to engage your children in these activities will not only develop them in physical ways, but you will also develop their ability to express ideas and creativity to audiences without fear. The more comfortable your children become in their own skin at an early age, the more confidence and strength they will develop to express their true selves.

Developmental Outcomes for Preadolescent Children

Your children will continue to make developmental strides as you remain actively involved in their lives. You want to consistently gauge their abilities and interests through your interactions and time spent in home-work tasks, and other social and recreational activities. As your children enter middle school, they will begin to identify interests, desires, and abilities in various social, physical, and educational activities.

Social and Emotional Development

By preadolescence, your children should be able to engage in competitive and non-competitive games, which include sports. To do so, they will be able to define and follow the rules of games and activities. They will be able to demonstrate the key virtues of patience, sharing, and respect for others' differences and points of view. Through your interactions from preschool age through the elementary school years, you want to ensure that your children's activities surround the use of books, engagement of people and activities. You should intro-duce them to many cultures to help them to embrace and celebrate the uniqueness not only for various cul-tures but for each individual. As your children learn to embrace their own uniqueness within their culture, they will begin to see that diversity goes beyond a cul-ture and moves more specifically to the celebration of the soul's desire. As a parent, you want to process the importance and beauty of each individual on the planet to help your child develop the social and emotional skills to engage every person with love and respect.

When you children understand the uniqueness and beauty possessed by all people, they will be better equipped to resolve conflicts and think critically. As you teach your children that life is filled with possibilities and ways to look at situations, they will be better able to see others' point of view and make decisions based upon the beliefs centered on hope, love, and joy. This is not to say that your children should ever abandon their beliefs and values when they encounter conflicts with others. By understanding that others also have a belief and value system that is as powerful and as real as theirs, your children must be able to allow others to come to their own conclusions over time on what beliefs serve them best. In the meantime, they need to develop the ability to show love and respect to any-one regardless of any differences. As a parent, you must also gauge your belief system to make sure that you understand this concept, so you do not instill beliefs in your children that introduce hate and prejudgment towards anyone that is different from them. This is why you must find your way to happiness by tracing back to where you ran off the tracks and began to feel emotions of anger and hate. You do not want your children to adopt the same thoughts and beliefs that brought you to a negative place in your life.

Physical Development

By this stage of development, your preadolescent children should be able to differentiate between a quiet and high energy activity. They should be able to throw and catch a ball and demonstrate an ability to tumble, jump, and balance their weight by walking on a balance beam and by riding a bicycle. In addition, they should also develop the ability to swim and float in water. Children that do not learn these skills begin to place barriers to engaging in physical and social activities with peers and gain the tendency to remain indoors and isolated from other children. These children also find themselves very anxious about attending physical education classes in school as they do not possess the basic throwing, catching, and coordination skills in basic gymnastic maneuvers. As a parent, you will want to expose your children to physical and recreational activities to develop these skills, which keeps them socially engaged with peers. When children find fun and excitement in physical activity, they gain a belief that physical exercise is of benefit and are more likely to continue to engage in some form of physical activity through adolescence.

Mental Development

Rapid cognitive growth creates many of the positive as well as negative social interactions between children and adults during middle childhood. You can help your children develop their thinking and processing skills by including them is solving issues in the home regarding scheduling activities, division of chores and other negotiable issues. Organizational skills are very important at this stage of development, so your ability to assist your children in understanding how to prioritize and sequence "things to do" to meet deadlines through lists and other journaling methods will be very important.

Helping your children process their day at the dinner table is a key way to support and model mental and social negotiation skills. As your children acclimate to speaking of the positive and challenging parts of their day regarding teachers, peers, and siblings, you can provide a forum for problem solving. Assist your children in processing information and developing positive thinking and behavioral strategies to manage challenging issues, keeping in mind that your children may avoid responsibility for any actions or emotional responses on their part. Since projecting blame is a common practice of preadolescents, you will want to remind your children that their behavior and emotions are always a choice and cannot be projected on another person. As your children consistently hear this message, they will learn accountability and responsibility.

Teens

Each stage in life is a time of growth. Preadolescence to adolescence is a time to bridge your children's dependence with approaching independence. Their time of wonder and spontaneity is being invaded by negative messages of other students placing pressure on your children to feel self-conscious and on guard. Your children will start to identify areas of future potential in their academic, physical, and social life domains. In essence, your children begin to develop and find their identity from this point through adolescence. As a parent, you may find yourself very challenged by some of your children's thoughts regarding their potential and future. You must always parent from a position of love and avoid some of the pitfalls to parenting preadolescent and adolescent kids. The first pitfall to avoid is criticism and comparison. Your teenage children are very aware and overly self-conscious about the way they think, feel, and look. They really do not need you to point out your perception of personal flaws. Always encourage and model physical activity and good eating habits. These activities help your teenagers look and feel their best while providing much needed energy release and relaxation to ensure well-being.

As a parent, do not shy away from discussions with your teenagers regarding sex. The more information that you provide, the more secure your children will feel about the changes in their body during adolescence. Discussion surrounding sex does not encourage sexual activity. In fact, the more information and answers that you provide about the issues surrounding sexuality, the better prepared your children will be to adopt beliefs in line with your views regarding sexuality and morality. When you deny that your children will not think about sex or have sexual urges, you only ensure that your teenagers will keep you out of the loop in their pursuit of answers to their questions When friends and other media become their main source of processing critical information, your teenagers may adopt thoughts and beliefs that are counter to yours. Relax! Your children will not want to spend too much time on this subject area with you. As a parent, you want your children to know that you are approachable and interested in their overall health and well-being, which includes sexuality. There are single parents that feel uncomfortable speaking to their children of opposite genders, In these cases, find a trusted person that shares your beliefs to provide this assistance to ensure your teenagers have a way to process the changes in their bodies during puberty and beyond. Accurate information is all that your teenagers are asking for when they ask questions about sexuality. It is when children get inaccurate information from other kids when bad decisions can occur.

Allow your teenager some space and do not take it personally if their affection for you appears to be waning. Teens need some time to separate from parents as they are developing independence. Respect this need for some space and allow for your teenagers to make decisions on whether or not to hug or kiss you or other relatives. Teenagers have mixed emotions regarding their need for parents as they begin to feel more aligned with their age group, which sometimes leads to their ignoring parental advice. The best approach from a parent is to allow for some flexibility and to demonstrate patience. This patience will come in handy as your teens start to take excessive time in the bathroom with their grooming habits. Your teenagers are just trying to gain some control of a body that is changing at such a rapid rate. Again, your love and encouragement are all that is needed, so refrain from criticism and sarcasm as these can cause your teenagers to experience additional stress and anxiety. As you praise your child's efforts and positive habits, she will be more likely to stick with them and keep you in the loop of what she is thinking during those days when she experiences apprehension about her world.

Since your teenagers are on the path to adulthood, you want to provide opportunities for them to participate in the development of their rules and consequences for activities outside of your supervision. These activities would include friends and eventually dating relationships. Part of this negotiation should include your input on ways trust will remain in place. You want to negotiate how plans and curfews will be established along with how changes in plans get communicated. As a parent, you must allow your teenagers to experience independence outside and inside the home. As long as you continue to be significant to your children, they will continue to communicate with you openly and honestly. Allow your teenagers to participate in daily living skills in the home, which include laundry, cooking, and cleaning. Provide the support and mentoring to allow your children to gain mastery of the skills that you possess with daily living. Open up a checking account for your teenagers as they begin to earn money from part-time jobs or allowances that you may provide.

One of the best ways for your teenagers to gain valuable work skills is through community service. Not only will they develop vocational and social skills, your teenagers' efforts will also be recognized by universities and foundations that award grants and scholarships. Teenagers experience situations that identify interests and preferences when they engage in community service. Their ability to define interests and abilities helps to further define their future pursuits. These experiences can reinforce the work that you and your children engaged in developing their desires and yearning in life.

Your teens will want to become involved in activities where they can contribute and find deeper meaning. By working with the less fortunate, they can develop their ability to love and respect others. This also helps to provide a framework around the concept of appreciation. During the course of your children's journey, they will need to develop their ability to take pause and reflect on their blessings in life. This sole behavior will ground them and bring them back from any negativity surrounding their perception of not having those things they desire leading him down the path to negativity.

One of the critical aspects of teenage development centers on self-discovery. Your teenagers must establish their own identities based upon what their soul has called them to be rather than adopting what everyone else is claiming to be. Over the course of the adolescent years, teens begin to integrate the opinions of influential others (e.g. parents, other significant adults, friends, etc.) into their own likes and dislikes. The eventual outcome is your child having a clear sense of their values and beliefs, occupational goals, and relationship expectations. People with secure identities know where they fit or where they don't want to fit in their world. Through your involvement and their exposure to many different experiences in life, your teenagers will find their identity much easier than children that did not have the exposure and belief system that reinforce concepts, such as there are endless possibilities in life and that the world is safe and abundant with resources and opportunities. Along with an identity, your teen will need to develop autonomy. Some people assume that autonomy refers to becoming completely independent from others, which is inaccurate. Rather than severing relationships, however, establishing autonomy during the teen years really means becoming an independent and self-governing person within relationships. Autonomous teens have gained the ability to make and follow through with their decisions, live by their own beliefs of right and wrong, and have become less emotionally dependent on parents. Autonomy is necessary if the teen is to become self-sufficient and happy.

Teenagers Becoming Adults

By the time your children enter the teen years, they will begin to express more of who they are in the way they talk, dress, and act. Their friends will also represent many of their interests and core values. As a parent, your new belief system will undergo testing as you may attempt to inhibit your children's need to express themselves and expand in many areas to further define their path and life journey. The truth is that your children's passions need to be the driving force behind the meaning and purpose to which they place on their present and future path. The only way that they will find happiness and fulfillment is when they encounter social, recreational, and educational activities that progress their desires and interests towards their purpose and calling in life. Their journey to their life purpose should not impede on the rights of others nor should it compromise their health and safety. Taking illegal substances is not a life purpose. Any activity that compromises their desire, enthusiasm, or health is not driven by love and passion for life.

Parents tend to influence their children's decisions and interests at this stage of development. If your children are raised to be present in the moment and not made to feel doubt, guilt, or worry about what others think, they will be better able to define and pursue their interests and passions that were acquired over the years of exposure to people, places, and activities. If your children are riddled with guilt, worry, and doubt, then they believe that other people's opinions matter more than theirs and that their decisions need the approval of others. As a parent, you need to be aware of this as you are the teacher and enforcer of this belief system. Although this is a late stage of development to introduce new belief systems, you want to instill beliefs that your children's decisions should be based upon autonomous thinking. Your children can always ask for an opinion about a decision. This keeps the decision and choices in your children's control.

Parents also need to be aware of their own belief system and what type of language they use to communicate with their children. Your children's language is a good way to gauge the beliefs held and level of happiness or unhappiness that is present in their lives. Much of our language brings out our unconscious beliefs without our knowing. If you and your teenager begin to take note of the messages that you convey on a regular basis, you will discover the barriers to your happiness and outcomes desired in life. Do you communicate joy, hope, love, and infinite possibilities, or do you put yourself down, talk about problems, complain, blame, or discuss impossibilities? Teenagers tend to run the gambit of emotions during the explosion of hormonal changes in the body, so emotional highs and lows will occur. Teenagers will show a baseline level of well-being in which they either show excitement and enthusiasm for life or more fear and frustration toward people, places, and activities. As a parent, you want to be aware and responsive to your children through compassion and love by demonstrating understanding and kindness. The last thing your child needs is critical feedback. Do not worry; as you remain present with your children and offer love and compassion, they will want to hear your opinions. The key is to be present and patient.

If our present thoughts become future things in our lives based upon the workings of the subconscious mind and universal laws, then our words are another extension of our thinking. When we speak of being old, tired, sick, weak, depressed, or any other negative message, we send this message to our subconscious that goes to work to ensure that this becomes our reality. Do your children complain about relationships and the academics in school? Do they complain of being tired, depressed, or worried about their future? Do they put themselves down and emphasize perceived weaknesses? As a parent, you do not want to pressure your child to adopt a new view or look at any thought or belief. You want to explore the situations surrounding the negative emotions and allow your children to see how their perception of the situation can be looked at differently.

If you use force or any means that provoke guilt and doubt to attempt to change their thoughts or beliefs, then your teenagers will experience more momentum in their downward spiral. The key is to validate your teenager's feelings as they are real and serve a purpose. As a parent, you then can assist your children to refocus on what they want based upon their unwanted experiences. The key is to not remain focused on what is unwanted as this just feeds negative emotions.

You and your children will live the type of life revealed through your words or thoughts and images that signify what you want or do not want. As you both reinforce the things you do not want or your qualities that are lacking, the more these perceived weaknesses or problem issues will show up in your lives as your subconscious mind will go to work to project these images to you. There are countless times when we make statements about others and ourselves that have reinforced a very negative image. When we make negative statements about ourselves or others, we do so with great emotion, which really wakes up the subconscious mind to capture the sentiment and make this our new belief or reinforce a reoccurring thinking pattern. Monitor your teenagers' communications. If they are placing more emphasis on problems, negative physical traits, and barriers to life, you will need to begin to provide support. Your compassion and love to assist them, is very important. Help them to shift their beliefs to ones involving finding solutions to challenges, identifying positive attributes, knowing there are infinite possibilities, and allowing in the love of others. The more that you present happiness, joy, and love to your teenagers, the better chance they will have in modifying their thinking to more positive alternatives.

Healing Self-Esteem

In the teenage years, your children, and maybe even you, may suffer from a wounded self-esteem. There are different types of wounds that impact our perception of our self-worth. Our worth becomes wounded when we are not aligned with the belief that we our worthy of anything we want regardless of our actions and recognitions. The first area in which children invite an attack on self-esteem is when they allow others' words and deeds to negatively impact their perceived worth as a human being. This is the typical way that self-esteem is targeted by bullies and is very prevalent in schools and other child and teen activities. As discussed, your children's belief system influences how they manage the communications from others. This includes the communication that impacts their esteem. When children develop the belief that their value is not a product of the opinion of others, then their interactions with others automatically are enhanced with confidence and high self-esteem.

Fear is the driving emotion for esteem issues for children and adults. From the beginning of this book, the emotion of fear is said to be the fuel of the ego and the cause of our negative outlook on life. The kids who are picked on along with the bullies who pick on them are both running on the emotion of fear. This is why they are both drawn to each other. As an adult, this is why abusers and the abused are drawn together. This universal law of attraction is being revealed more and more as a scientific, psychological, and spiritual truth. For your children to be ready to go out into the world, they must be driven by love and compassion. If not, their presentation to others will be easily perceived as defensive and more insecure, which are what negative emotions present to our psyche.

The bully profile can also be one that develops from a perceived low esteem. Children who engage in bullying behavior can also possess an inflated self-esteem. The second type of esteem involves children who have been told that they possess skills and abilities, yet in reality, these skills were never fully developed. Many children are told that they are great at sports, reading, writing, art, and other activities without demonstrating skill mastery and aptitudes. Without feedback and encouragement to work on skill development, the same children develop a narcissistic outlook in which they begin to realize their deficiencies and fear the consequences if others discover their shortcomings. Initially, the child feels good when praised for effort and participation. Parents should encourage children to try new activities and engage others in a multitude of situations that promote physical, spiritual, emotional, and intellectual stimulation. The encouragement should be offered to help children develop interests and build the skills to progress in any areas of interest. Your encouragement should also serve for your children to discover that certain interests are not realistic to pursue because of their lack of interest, and/or abilities.

Today, society is placing more emphasis on all children being grouped as the same while not being presented an honest picture of their development needs. In sporting events, many recreational centers and organizations have "no win" policies while providing all participants with messages that they demonstrate great ability. On the surface, their intentions are good, yet the child who lacks ability is not provided the honest feedback and development path to become better. There are parents who do spend time with their child in developing the skills necessary. Many children are brought through early development, believing they possess more ability than they do. In school, the curriculum is based upon the less-able student, which does little to help bring ability up to higher standards to keep many children of higher ability stimulated and challenged.

As some of the children develop and enter adolescence with all the accolades and praises of possessing abilities and skills that are really not present, they develop an insecure and fearful state of being. These children develop egos that go to every extent to protect them from being discovered by others for their inability to perform. Some of these children become very frustrated and angry when their deficiencies are brought forth in front of their peer group. To compensate for these strong feelings of vulnerability and insecurities, the children with inflated esteems turn to children with low esteems and inflict emotional and/or physical harm. In middle school, there are more reports of the popular and so-called normally adjusted kids bullying kids with low self-esteem. The narcissistic adolescent is attempting to regain control and power to counter the fears that they possess.

When children with narcissistic tendencies enter college and discover the high level of academic skill in their peer group, many ego responses can occur. The most common ego response is for these college students to turn to drug abuse and other distracting behaviors. Their attempt is to mask the pain and fear experienced with the realization that they are not the smartest or best looking or most charming. The dropout rate at universities continues to be great for freshmen who cannot adjust to the environment of academic high achievement. Since these children did not discover their true purpose from an honest assessment of abilities and interests, they find themselves lost and scared about what steps to take while transitioning to adulthood. To avoid pain, frustration, and anxiety, their ego will guide them to project blame outwardly. Although they want to be a high achiever, their ego takes over and does not easily allow them to come to the truth. The longer children are reinforced for skills and abilities not possessed, the more difficult it becomes for them to take responsibility for thinking and acting in ways to meet desires and goals.

In essence, the inflated esteem of children result in a low esteem; however, the difference is their denial and ability to accept the truth about their true present attributes and abilities. The parenting role is crucial to ensure children find their way in a loving and fulfilling way. By supporting your children and helping them to develop interests along with skills, you will ensure that they gain a realistic picture of what they can do and what truly interests them. With your loving support, you must also be honest with your children as to their abilities and needs to meet development milestones. If your child does not show much ability in certain physical, social, and intellectual areas, you need to communicate this. The key is how you do so and the support that you provide in the development of the skills. The three elements that need to be present with your interactions with your child are love, respect, and honesty.

Through your love, you want to support and encourage your child to engage in as many activities as possible to help them develop academic, vocational, physical, and social skills. While engaging in these activities, you will want to provide constructive feedback on their performance, utilizing communication that demonstrates respect and honesty. This communication should allow for you to present the positive aspects of your child's willingness to engage in a new activity. The next step is communicating what steps your children need to follow in order to fully develop necessary skills. You also want to communicate your commitment in supporting this development. This communication provides the encouragement and next steps to your children as they become more aware of what is involved in the progression of the skill in which they show interest.

Many children with inflated esteems are given the impression that they already demonstrate proficiency in skill areas through encouragement, yet they are not provided honest feedback as to the progressive steps to skill development and mastery. With children making the decision to refrain from working any harder or further in the area, they remain insufficiently trained and underdeveloped in the skill area, creating a gap in their perceived skills and actual skills. When these kids enter middle and high schools, their egos take a big hit when they see that others perform at a higher level in physical education, academics, and social situations. To attempt to fit in and regain control of their environment, they do anything to be considered part of the in-crowd even if this means taking on the personality of the popular kids. Many times this includes taunting and teasing the kids who are different and more vulnerable.

As a parent, you need to nurture your children's pursuit of interests and vocations in life. If you do not know ways in which you can support your children in the pursuit of their interests and passions, join them to research ways to progress their skill and interest areas. You can also work with professionals as life coaches are available to help children and parents find their path to fulfilling dreams and yearnings. As mentioned, reading, writing, and arithmetic mastery is very necessary for your child to move forward in life. If you do not possess skills in these areas, find folks who can assist in this skill development with your children. The only way that your children can progress toward their desires and dreams is if they can develop the skills necessary to pursue any dream, which include academic, spiritual, physical, emotional, and social skills. The mind, body, and spirit of your children must be developed to ensure that your children understand their true power in creating the life that they can conceptualize and desire. Instill the belief that the pursuit of knowledge is a life long process.

You are a very important component to your children's development. Your ability to instill and nurture a belief system surrounding possibilities, abundance, and safety is paramount in dispelling fear and doubt in your children. You play an important teaching and modeling role as you introduce activities and experiences to your children that support social, academic, physical, and spiritual development. Throughout the developmental stages, you want to remain a significant part of their lives while helping them develop autonomy. The best gift you can bestow on your children is the gift of allowing them to find their path free from guilt and fear. You can still support your children's dreams while helping them to honestly assess their abilities, which will help their esteem remain high and not inflated. Your children's path to greatness is inspired by their knowing that the journey is well worth the time and effort for the end result will provide great meaning and fulfillment. Remember those times when you engaged in activities that brought you happiness and joy. The actions that you took to bring about the end results of happiness and joy did not feel like work, and time stopped while you were engaged in the activity. When your children find a true calling and desire in life, their skill development and journey toward this calling will not feel burdensome as the progression to this purpose is a great part of the pleasure and enjoyment of life.

Faith in Action

What brings parenting with soul and dream fulfillment to a reality is the concept of faith. What is faith?
Knowing what is not yet proved to be so or believing
in things not seen are some initial definitions of faith.
Faith is a key element to the entire process of finding
and acquiring your dreams and purpose in life. Faith
requires and reinforces the belief that each of you truly
know that you will acquire your desires before there is
any evidence as to how this will be achieved. Faith is one
of those words that either turns you on or off, depend-
ing on your understanding and belief in the power of
this concept. The fact of the matter is that everyone who
has attained their desires in life had believed ahead of
time that they would. Happy and successful people see
the end result without getting caught up in processes
and the "how tos" in the initial path to the goal. When
you walk through the activities that involve assessing
and building powerful life-changing beliefs and start
to focus on new positive and empowering ones, your
understanding of faith will slowly begin to take hold.

Once a desire and strong calling in life is identified
during your journey and your child's development, the

next step is to go right to the finish line and imagine what the end result would be. The more you imagine the places, people, smells, and sounds that surround your desire, the more emotion you will draw, which will make your subconscious mind believe that the desire has come to pass. Once you and your child's subconscious mind adopts these desires as present truths, you and your child will be inspired to act in ways that will bring you closer to your dreams. When one has total faith in an outcome that has not yet occurred, the excitement of the eventual attainment is heightened and the person of faith is inspired to take action. The circumstances and people who will assist in the attainment of the desire will find their way to both of you as long as you are making efforts to get out into the world and discuss your desires with others.

The key to fulfilling dreams is not to know all the steps and actions needed. The biggest step in the acquisition of your goal is defining what you desire and creating a belief system that insists that you will achieve it. Many people do not believe that the playing field is fair and also believe that special circumstances or luck is involved to cause certain people to achieve success. If you take a close look at people who succeed and realize dreams, you would see that each focused on the end result first. They were later inspired to act while finding people, places, and circumstances that came together to work out the details and complete their journey. Most of the time, the same people received more than they could ever hope to achieve and found that their purpose grew bigger than they could have ever imagined.

When you can raise your children to develop beliefs that empower them to think big and trust that people and circumstances will rally around them on their behalf, they will gain the confidence and strength to pursue dreams and dismiss feelings of doubt, fear, and frustration. Your children will start to view the world as giving and loving, which will fuel their own love and compassion for others. You and your child are more powerful than you have been taught. You control the outcomes of your experiences in the world. As you understand this and make this your belief, you will expand your confidence and knowledge as to how you can make the world fit your beliefs. Living each moment in the present is the first step to refocusing the mind to the desires that you have. As you stay present and work through those distracting beliefs that cause you anxiety, guilt, doubt, and worry, you will find that the only task for you or your child to partake is that task that will bring you the most excitement and joy.

As you engage in activities that bring you excitement and joy, you will start to move closer to the true you and begin to experience how acting on your passions moment by moment, day by day, will lead you to the people, places, and events that will bring you to what you truly desire. Children do this instinctively as they engage in play and activities that they find great pleasure and joy in until they are guided away from their fun through the introduction of beliefs of conforming to norms and parental expectations. As an adult, you may need to take some small steps in each moment to engage in activities and experiences that bring you joy and excitement. The best way is to break the routine and change things up so you can begin to ignite your senses and awareness of the present moment. You will be surprised at how much time your mind spends in the past and future. This is why these beliefs that lead you to worry, doubt, and guilt must be replaced with the thoughts of infinite possibilities of your passions and desires.

As you develop your skill to follow your joy and excitement in present moments, you and your children will want to make sure that you communicate your passions to the people who you engage with along the way. As each of you becomes more compassionate and excited about life and your passions, you will find more people and circumstances that will come into your life that will help you define and move toward your purpose and yearning in life. Each of you will begin to attract people who have similar interests. Some of these contacts could be your future partners helping you move toward what you want to achieve. The journey, if taken moment by moment with joy and excitement, will be just as gratifying as reaching the end desire. As mentioned, if you speak to people who are living their passion, they will tell you that the time moving to the end goal was the greatest part of ride! When you and your children know and believe that each of you will fulfill your purpose in life, you will find excitement in living each moment of your life. Each of these moments will contain more and more signs from people and places that your dream is getting closer, which will help you remain encouraged and hopeful. When you and your children are able to see your thoughts start to materialize into the form of expression that impacts others, you will understand how powerful your thoughts and beliefs are to creating the magic in your life.

The caveat that must be made here is that your pursuit of joy and excitement cannot impede on other's rights or hurt others or you. There is a difference between finding excitement and joy to discover your passion and purpose in life and performing acts that cause harm to others and/or yourself. You may find drug use exciting and joyful, but the long-term harm to you and others will bring more hurt and misery. There is a difference in seeking joy and excitement and attempting to escape anxiety and pain. We all want to feel good, and this is what drives us to act in any manner. Do purposeful activities to find your excitement by staying present in activities that help you see, touch, smell, hear, and taste the life in front of you. This starts the ball rolling to your discovery of the true you. Get away from the distractions of television, computer games, and other activities that numb the senses. Get outside and see life in action from all perspectives of nature. Teach your children to do the same as nature has much to teach them about the beauty and perfection of their world.

You may find this approach difficult and not rational in your pursuit of happiness. This approach will lead you and your children to your passions and life purposes. Each of you will spend more of your time engaged in activity centering on what you really enjoy and want to do in life. Your children do this joyful dance in the beginning stages of life for they look to each activity as an adventure and feel the excitement and thrill of being in the moment and taking full participation in all the activity brings. People notice those who have high energy and passions for what they do. This is why high excitement and joy attract the right people to help you move closer and closer to your desires. This is when your love for life and others begins to replace the fears that you once had, which kept you from engaging others in your natural state of being. When we are experiencing negative emotions, this is our indication that we are not allowing our natural state of love and well-being to occur.

Over time, the more you and your children think and believe in positive ways, all of your subconscious wirings will make these themes more prominent in your daily thoughts, feelings, and actions. Reprogramming your brain to adopt positive thoughts and beliefs takes a more conscious effort initially, especially if you have been practicing thoughts and beliefs that have left you feeling more negative than positive for many years. Your child will find this process automatic if positive thoughts and beliefs are established and maintained early in their development. The key is to be patient and not to be hard on yourself for feeling frustration, hurt, and pain. These emotions serve us well, especially in helping us to identify what we prefer and want as opposed to those things causing us pain and distress. Again, we need to honor and validate our feelings but not remain stuck in the negative emotions by finding more and more issues to pile on to continue the downward spiral.

There are many spiritual views on faith. Many of us claim to believe that we have faith that a higher power will take care of our needs but really do not submit to this belief as we fear our past, present, and future. There are psychological and scientific studies that reinforce the concept of faith. When we believe that we are in possession of our desires even though they have not yet materialized, we send our subconscious mind images and emotions that stimulate impulses for us to take action. There are universal laws that state that we do attract people and circumstances that match our thoughts and beliefs. When we begin to know that faith reinforces our new positive belief system, we can gain insight into how the world responds to us. We no longer react to the world with this new understanding. In fact, what we view in the world will take on more of what we believe.

Healthy and Happy Together

The bond that you will develop with your child as you both find your joy and happiness together will provide the glue to lifetime love. The most revealing truth about happiness is that this alone attracts all that you and your child will ever need to be fulfilled in life. All other desires will come to pass, and you will eventually come to know that money and material wealth is not what brings you the most joy. As you and your child find your calling in life, your ability to serve others with your talents and gifts will go much further to provide you with fulfillment and joy than any material purchase you will ever make. When you both begin to see this truth, you both will know what love truly is. You will both come to know love as your love for self will be reflected by the love that you experience from others.

As you and your child continue to practice living in each moment and acting upon your joy and excitement, you will find your relationships, health, and abundance in life improving. When you act on your passions and excitement, your presentation will become a magnet for others to join in and take part. Joyful people are attracted to people exhuming joy and happiness. Your joyous approach to life helps to bring momentum and additional support to the eventual ways that you and your child will define and access your true yearning and calling in life. We may have adopted beliefs that are in opposition to what has been outlined in this book. You may have been told that you need to work very hard and that only the few and fortunate ones make it big in life. If so, you must change this belief if you ever want to gain the momentum to follow your passions and make the journey to your dreams.

When you start out in this new direction, your tendency will be to revert back to old beliefs when fear and doubt creep in to your mind. Feelings of fear should never be denied, yet the thoughts behind the fear need to be evaluated to see what beliefs continue to be embraced by your conscious and subconscious mind. As stated, fear is based upon the ego attempting to separate you from the person that you truly are and keeps you from experiencing happiness and love. The ego attempts to convince you that you need to protect yourself from others and harm when in fact the ego, at times, places you in harm's way. Your feelings will guide all of you to how well your thoughts and beliefs are serving you. Positive feelings of hope, appreciation, joy, love, and compassion are signs that you are thinking and believing in truths that serve you well. When you feel suspicious of others or frustrated with someone, your actions can place in a power play with another that puts more risk for a negative outcome in the relationship. When you feel angry, hurt, frustrated, or even depressed, your presentation will place you in compromised position with others. Your negativity will result in strained and/or separated relationships. Your ability to take responsibility for your thoughts and feelings are very critical in making the shift to happier feelings. Your happiness should never be contingent upon anyone or anything but you! The only feelings that bring sustained happiness are love and compassion.

As you and your child continue to follow the path to your joy and excitement in life, there will be those who will object to your new beliefs and thought processes. Many friends and family members will continue to inject old beliefs and thinking during your interactions. Although many will mean well, they will attempt to introduce guilt, doubt, and fear to your thinking. As you find more evidence that your path is leading you to your joy and happiness, you will be better able to resist their persistence that you go back to perceiving life through the lenses of lack and fear. Remain present and allow others to be who they are without allowing them to impact your thoughts and beliefs regarding your path in life. You and your child must learn to enjoy having these interactions and sharing ideas while agreeing to disagree. You both will also attract a new sphere of friends who will support and encourage your new strategies for living life.

Do not allow others to victimize you. Victimization is a strong word but a useful one. You and your children can allow others to victimize each of you if each of you are not able to internalize new beliefs that empower rather than weaken. At some point, we all have chosen to allow others to victimize us in our lives and have gone as far as to use this victimization to serve a purpose for us. A strong belief that many of us adopt is that change is difficult and scary. The known, even when hurtful and/or stifling, is what we chose many times to avoid new challenges in our lives. Your child will not start off with these fears, so until you get a grip on your fear of change, you will need to be vigilant to ensure your own fear of change does not influence you from allowing your child to experience different experiences for growth and exploration.

When you or your child allow others to make either of you doubt your decision to seek your highest joy, you are both choosing the path of victimization. How many times have you thought of something that inspired you, only to be talked out of pursuing this dream? Did you find out later that someone else who was no more skilled than you accomplished a similar feat? What you believe internally is what you get externally in your life. When you begin to understand the power you truly possess to acquire what you want, you will be more willing to unleash your true potential. Each of you will discover a world that wants to clear the path for you. The success gurus talk about being in the right state of mind to make things happen in life. This state comes from a belief that you can obtain what you want no matter what path is needed. Your paths may change several times as you take your journey to your highest yearning. In the end, none of us ever reach all of what we want, but would that be as fun as the excitement of the chase?

Parenting a child to understand the infinite possibilities in life is a crucial role for a parent. Too many children grow up in families with limiting beliefs and preconceived ideas. Some of these ideas present that the game of life is rigged and their kids will lose before they get out of the starting gate. A child's natural inclination is to think big and see all kinds of possibilities as imagination is part of the everyday experience. You and your child see life from a brain that projects what you believe to be true. Although we may be able to agree on many of the images that we all see from a given vantage point, there are enough variations on how images, smells, tastes, and sounds are perceived to show that our realities are different. You know for yourself that there are days when all is right in the world and that there is very little anyone can do to make you see them in a negative way, while there are other days when there is very little that you find right in the world. The world did not change, yet you changed how the world looked based upon the beliefs and thoughts you embraced that day. The better that you and your child become at developing and maintaining beliefs based upon love and compassion, the brighter and more joyful your world will become.

Maintaining newly formed beliefs will come with challenges. The more that you and your children remain committed to working on their thoughts and beliefs, the better able each of you will become to avoid pitfalls that bring back old patterns where others sway any of you from your dreams. Many of us have become used to playing the role of victim or martyr. These roles are reinforced by others through pity and even admiration. To move from these roles, we must see that change and the unknown are part of the exciting journey of our lives. By adopting similar positive beliefs, you and your children can maintain a connection of love to weather all storms and share in each other's happiness.

Maintaining the Real Self through Strength and Love

The easy road in life may seem to be the path of resisting change and maintaining the status quo. As a matter of fact, we are supposed to sacrifice and suffer while on this earth, right? Resisting your natural tendency to love, evolve, and act in your true nature will take more effort than taking the path of least resistance where your true nature wants to laugh, love, and find peace with others. Each time you act in loving and joyful ways, you gain more strength and infuse life to your persona. There is an easy path of conforming to what others' want from you, which ends up becoming a harder road to live as you feel negativity and boredom. Your strength to act on your greatest joy and yearning in life is very important, so you can face your lingering fears that contribute to beliefs that opinions of others mean more than your own thoughts and actions.

To continue your journeys, you and your child must be trendsetters and innovators in life. By following your callings and desires in life, you will be led to people, places, and events that will help you to gather the resources to make your joy and passions come to life. Along the way, you most likely will face obstacles that can be viewed as challenges or problems based upon what you both continue to believe to be true in your life. Strength and courage must comprise your new belief system where you both place your faith in yourselves. Know that your passions and yearnings will yield you all that you will need to be happy and abundant in life. If the truth be told, you will know this to be the case as long as your courage keeps you living moment by moment. Past and future thinking usually brings fear back to your experience where the ego makes its case to go back to the way that it has always been.

The key is to meet at least one person who shares in your passion, which will help each of you remain enthusiastic and joyful during the initial steps toward your goal. By staying positive and hopeful, each of you will attract other like-minded people who will help start the momentum of finding the joy and meaning in life that each of you so want and deserve. Through your initial tests of strength and courage to follow your dreams, each of you will develop a loving network of friends who will assist in opening the doors to other people and resources in which your dreams will unfold. All you ever need to do is to share your passion with others along the way, and the magic will begin to reveal more of the steps that will catapult you to your dreams. Each of you will meet one person after another who will provide contacts and resources to get your dream to manifest. As more people share in the discussion of what you really want in life, your dream will begin to be defined in more specifics. Each of you will learn how your yearning can be materialized into something tangible for others to benefit.

You and your child truly live in a magical world when you learn how the universe works to give you what you want in life. You and your child are uniquely blessed with talents and passions that are valuable to others. People love those who share their talents with passion. People in the community are eager to provide assistance and resources to help make the dreams occur. You must understand that there are so many people out in the world wanting to help and assist your family members in whatever dream each of you may have. Have the strength and conviction to go out and let others into your life, and make your claim on their generosity. In return, your family members must also make your mission to serve others with your talents and help others to develop their passions. By serving and loving others, you are reinforcing the positive belief system that you are putting in place. The flow of love you are giving and receiving will be a continuous loop. Your conscious and subconscious mind will reinforce the truth that love and abundance are in your world.

As you and your child continue to move closer to your dreams, take time to observe nature and the world around you. Look at the grass, stream, lake, flowers, trees, and sky. You may notice the beauty of nature for the first time as you begin to find love and peace in your life. When you live a life of love rather than fear, the beauty of people and nature will begin to shine through your eyes as your new mind will see new frames to the movie of your world. You hear in spiritual texts about a rebirth and new world. This is the world you once knew as a young child who did not know about fear. Everything was clear and bright, and everyone was beautiful. Haven't you ever thought about why you are here in this world? Did you ever wonder what the meaning of life truly is before drifting off to sleep? You and your child did not just come into this world randomly and by accident. You both came into the world to create and experience an ever-expanding you with all the wonderful diversity of styles.

Part of your journey is to be able to remain focused on your wants and desires while allowing others to make the choices on the paths they will choose to follow. Your life experience can drift away from your dreams when you attempt to change others into adopting your new positive approaches to life. Many people who develop new skills and approaches attempt to share their new approaches with others only to find opposition and criticalness regarding their new insights. In this process, you can allow their negativity to deflate your enthusiasm and cause old beliefs to surface associated with past fears, doubts, and anxiety. This is not to say that you will not be able to discuss your experiences and new beliefs with others. You will attract like-minded people over time, which will feed your enthusiasm and share your optimistic approaches to living life.

The better approach is to model a life of strength and love. Others will notice and eventually want to know what you are doing to create such joy and enthusiasm for life. Your compassion and kindness will bring others closer to you, and over time, you will be able to share some of your new thoughts and beliefs. Many may not be able to conceive your beliefs, but they will not be able to deny that your beliefs are serving you well. By allowing others to be who they are and sharing your views when asked, you will remain in a better position to remain grounded in your new belief system. As you remain consistent in your positive approaches to living the life you want, you will develop the ability to discuss your approaches and beliefs with even the most negative people. You will joyfully do so and not be negatively impacted by their criticalness or opposition. You will have learned that you are not defined by others and that you do not seek approval. Your only driving force is to serve others and project love to them regardless of how your messages are received. More times than not, your messages will be respected as long as you can remain loving and not reactive to negativity.

The great news is that you and your child will have a relationship based upon a belief system that places love, joy, abundance, and happiness in the forefront. You both will share in a life where all things are possible. You both will live a life full of the passion and love each of you always dreamed of, where laughter is a common occurrence and fun and excitement rules each day. You will both come to know that you can choose to make any situation better simply by how either of you decide to perceive it. The more that you experience the synchronicities in life, which assist you in obtaining your desires, the more that you will come to understand that are no accidents to living life. You and your child will come to know that people have a purpose to their lives and control the experiences. There are no mistakes in the human race. Each and every person is precious and made the decision to come forth by choosing their parents before conception even occurred.

When you see life as a choice, even prior to being born, you begin to strip away even more fear from your life and your existence. The beautiful children who are classified as "disabled" in some manner come to us to help each and every one of us to discover the unconditional love that we may have resisted yet desperately needed to find in order to unlock our own happiness. If you observe children with so-called special needs, you discover quickly that each live with passion and enthusiasm and most only find discontentment when others restrict their need for expression. We all must understand that everyone possesses unique gifts and talents. As a parent, you certainly need to embrace the uniqueness and special qualities your child brings to the world. From all the people in the world, your children chose you as the vehicle to come into this world and knew that you were the best person to support them in discovering their purpose in life.

When you find those times when you are feeling down and out, look your children right in their eyes. Feel how much they are a part of you for they already know you are a part of them. This is why your children want and need your time and attention as they see you both as one. Even though they will grow and develop into a person that may physically leave your presence for extended periods of time, your children will always be connected to you and will want to know you love them. As each of you reach your goals and find your purposes in life, each family member will come to understand that you all were just looking to love and be loved as this is what each of you at one time knew, but had forgotten. Do not allow your life to be filled with fear and anguish based on stuff that does not matter. Anything outside of love really does not even exist. Live each day, moment by moment, and relish time with each and every person that you encounter, even the most challenging folks. Bless your adversaries as they bring you closer to understanding your beliefs and the areas of your life to address. The day you make the shifts in your beliefs, your adversaries just vanish from your existence.

Keep your sense of humor, and laugh each day with your family, friends, and children. Laughter opens the door to love, so make fun a common occurrence as this reinforces your strength and love for life. Life was not meant to be difficult and so serious. Start believing that life was meant to be fun, and start looking at life as you did as a child. Understand that no setback lasts forever, so each day starts anew and brings so many great possibilities to you and your child. Live life from the inside out for you decide how to look at any situation and circumstance with the understanding that you and everyone else is eternal. What is better than that?

When you are all alone and allow your thoughts to calm, have you ever wondered why you have come to exist in the world. Have you looked at how the earth and the universe interact and wonder what keeps this all together? Have you ever wondered how you came to be able to create another life? As a child, you may have entertained more questions about the wonders of the world. By now, you may just accept the fact that life is all happenstance and can be explained by science. After this journey with your child, my hope is that you are finding that inner child in you and start to regain the ability to see and appreciate how perfect the world you live truly is. Sure, there may be societal challenges and people that need to find their true path in life, yet your experiences were meant to bring you back to love and to be the perfect nurturer and supporter of your greatest creation. You are contemplating or deciding to raise a child because this beautiful little soul promotes love from the beginning of life together through the rest of your lives. Your love will be challenged and magnified throughout your journey with your child. No other relationship will compare as this relationship was born out of your desire and nurtured by you.

By now, you have come to know that the way that you and your child thinks and believes impact both of your realities, as well as, your emotional and physical well being. Hopefully, you also noticed that the beliefs regarding the views of the world presented to you by your parents, teachers, friends, and others in your life may not be serving you well. The best way to find your truth is to challenge and seek information on any subject area from all angles and points of view. As a child, you naturally did this but soon learned that disagreement with authority brought you swift punishment and pressure to fall in line with the authority's beliefs and views of the world. Our political and educational systems present information from a particular point of view. These systems fail to include other perspectives from folks that were all part of the information and history of the past and current times surrounding topics being presented. The final challenges presented to you and your child is to develop and maintain your ability to think critically and feel compassionately. Too many of us today settle for the idea that there is not much that can be done to solve the challenges of the world or think that challenges are for others to think about and manage. Your actions would not and should not be to approach challenges with force or negative activities towards others on any troublesome issue in the world. When you partake in activities that cause you to become frustrated or overwhelmed, you lose your focus and your source of personal power. What you can do is become aware of the truth about your world and live the example of love and happiness that will be passed down to your child. It is the collective consciousness regarding the truth about the world and the treatment of humans in the history of the world that will create the shift from the separatism many of us feel today to a "oneness" that will create a better world.

When you look into your children's eyes, you want to know that they are aware of the world they live but also in love with where they desire the world to evolve. Their destiny will fall somewhere in the path of changing the world for the better. They will accomplish this by contributing their talents from their spirit to ensure their soul's desire shines a light that brings others closer to discovering who they are. When you have been the beneficiary of the talents of others that create music and art, do you not find those moments when you are swept away, if only for a moment, to come to know happiness and well-being? When you find the conveniences brought by the inventions of our time, do you not breathe a little easier knowing that you have easy access to all that you need every day? By helping others with your talents, you and your children will be part of the betterment of every person that you serve, which is how you can make the difference in this world and find your meaning and purpose in the process. By understanding your world and adopting the beliefs that serve you well, both you and your children will be able to bring out your best and continue to evolve to that person you were born to be.

In order for your world to get better, you must learn from your past and come to know all the great possibilities that are here right now. See yourself doing great things each and every day even if you do not feel good. Make it a point to tell someone that you love them each day along with yourself. Perform a kind act each day no matter how big or small. Learn to write love notes to others and letters of encouragement. The power of kindness and compassion will bring love to your thinking and shift you away from negative thinking. Stay focused on being a responsible and respectful person even when the easier act would be to check out, blame, criticize, or belittle. Spend your day in activities that bring you joy, laughter, and excitement. Fun activities do not require anything but your ability to be like your child. Life does not need to be a serious proposition, especially when you truly believe that all is well and will always be well throughout this life and all eternity!

The one truth to remember is that everything you experience in life is a reflection of what you believe to be true, so believe in love and happiness and what brings you the highest joy with all your might, your heart, and your soul!

Bibliography

Gregg Braden, *The Isaiah Effect: Decoding the Lost Science of Prayer and Prophecy.* New York: Three Rivers Press, 2000.

Eric Butterworth, *In the Flow of Life.* Unity Village, Missouri: Unity Books, 2011.

Jack Canfield and D.D. Watkins, *Key to Living the Law of Attraction: A Simple Guide to Creating the Life of Your Dreams.* Deerfield Beach, Florida: Health Communications, Inc., 2007.

Harry Carpenter, *The Genie Within: Your Subconscious Mind, How It Works and How to Use It.* Fallbrook, California: Harry Carpenter Publishing, 2011.

Mike Dooley, *Manifesting Change: It Couldn't Be Easier.* New York: Atria Paperback, 2010.

Mike Dooley, *Infinite Possibilities: The Art of Living Your Dreams.* New York: Atria Paperback, 2009.

Dr. Wayne W. Dyer, *Your Erroneous Zones: Step by Step Advice for Escaping the Trap of Negative Thinking and Taking Control of Your Life*, First HarperPerennial edition, 1991.

Ester and Jerry Hicks, *Learning to Manifest Your Desires*. Hay House, Inc., 2013.

Napoleon Hill, *Think and Grow Rich*. Lexington, Kentucky: Tribeca Books, 2013.

Joseph Murphy, *The Power of Your Subconscious Mind*. Radford, Virginia: Wilder Publications, 2007.

Anthony Robbins. "The 6 Human Needs: Why We Do What We Do," Robbins Research International, Inc., 2013. http://training.tonyrobbins.com/the-6-human-needs-why-we-do-what-we-do/.

Dr Judith Wright and Dr. Bob Wright, *Transformed!: The Science of Spectacular Living*. Turner, 2012.

Wikipedia, List of Child Prodigies. http://en.wikipedia.org/wiki/List_of_child_prodigies.

Marianne Williamson, *A Return to Love: Reflections on the Principles of A Course In Miracles*. HarperCollins Publishers, 1992.